Guide & Manual for Women's Home & Foreign Mission Society

2013

Program Materials for Senior Women's Auxiliary

Also Contains Constitution and Instructions for the Mothers' Union and Bible Band

* * * *

www.rhboydpublishing.com

6717 Centennial Blvd.
Nashville, Tennessee 37209

Table of Contents

SECTION I

Weekly Program Material: Women's Home and Foreign Missionary Society

First Quarter 2013

AREA:
The Ten Commandments

QUARTERLY THEME:
Famous Passages in the Bible

LESSONS FOR JANUARY—MARCH

January 6, 2013: Divine Priority
Exodus 20:1-3

"You shall have no other gods before me." (Exod. 20:3, NIV)

Whom do you worship? How do you find yourself spending times of worship? Are you worshiping God or is there someone or something else that has been taking precedence before God in your life? In Exodus, we learn Moses is given the Ten Commandments by God. These commandments are meant to teach God's children how to respect and worship Him and how to respect and treat each other. These laws were the first laws given to the Israelites, and they are still as essential today as they were then. These laws have not lost their importance through the years.

God brought His people out of Egypt, and He reminds the people of this in Exodus 20:2. Because He is their God, and He has saved them, God expects the Israelites not to put any other gods before Him. God is the only One we should worship. No one else and nothing else deserves our love and devotion.

Many things demand our time and attention these days. There are even people in our lives who insist on copious amounts of our time and devotion. Sometimes, there doesn't seem to be enough hours in the day to accomplish all that we need to. However, we must always make time for God—our only Father and Lord. He should be at the top of our list of priorities.

Activity: Begin to journal how you spend your time. Are praying, spending time with God, reading His Word, and sharing the Good News on your list?

January 13, 2013: No Idols

Exodus 20:4

"You shall not make for yourself an idol in the form of anything in heaven above or on the earth beneath or in the waters below." (Exod. 20:4, NIV)

When Moses returns from Mt. Sinai with the Ten Commandments for the first time, he finds the Israelites have constructed a golden calf, and they are worshiping it. Moses is furious. He throws "the tablets out of his hands, breaking them to pieces at the foot of the mountain" (Exod. 32:19, NIV). Then he burns the calf in a fire, destroying the false idol.

You might not have a golden calf in your home, but you might be surprised to learn that many items, including people, can become idols in your everyday life. If you were to list the five most important things that you need to function on a daily basis, would God make the list? Did your cell phone top the list? How about your husband, boyfriend, children, or best friends? Just because you use your cell phone every day, and possibly all day long, doesn't mean it's an idol, but we must all be careful to make sure it doesn't become one. Can you live without your cell phone? Yes. Can you live without God? No.

If you find there is an idol (or more than one) in your life, it's not too late to remove the idol and replace God in its spot. God should always be our number one. Yes, it's a fast-paced world, and yes, we have many demands placed on us, but there is always time and space for our number one—God.

Activity: Make a list of ways you can incorporate God in your day-to-day routines every single day. Make time for Him.

January 20, 2013: Worship No Others
Exodus 20:5-6

"But showing love to a thousand generations of those who love me and keep my commandments." (Exod. 20:6, NIV)

How many rules do you follow on a daily basis? Do you obey traffic laws? Do you follow the rules when it comes to work procedures? Do you listen to your college professors, guidance counselors, pastors, or more experienced elders? Although you might not realize it, you follow rules every day, even small rules. We wait to cross the street until we see the "Walk" sign. We drive on the right side of the road, and we use our turn signals to inform other drivers of our intentions.

How well do you obey God's commands? Do you refrain from worshiping idols? Do you listen to His voice when He speaks to you? God told the Israelites that He would give His love to everyone who loves Him and keeps His commandments. God has so much love to give, and He wants to bless us with His goodness. However, we must obey His commands.

The Ten Commandments are our beginning guidelines for how we can obey God. His commands will not only lead us to blessings, but they will also keep us out of danger. When we break God's commands, we hurt ourselves as well as others. God does not want His children to hurt. One simple way we can avoid unnecessary pain is by obeying God's commands.

Activity: Write down a list of rules you follow on a daily basis (you may be surprised at how many there are). Write down how well you obey God's commands. Discuss ways you can obey God in a more consistent manner.

January 27, 2013: Honor His Name
Exodus 20:7

"You shall not misuse the name of the LORD your God, for the LORD will not hold anyone guiltless who misuses his name." (Exod. 20:7, NIV)

God communicates with His people in different ways. One way He communicates with us is through His written Word. When we read the Bible, we can learn more about God, how to love Him, how to worship Him, and how to treat not only each other, but also God's world.

Not only does God's Word have power, but His name has great power, too. God tells His people not to misuse His name. You have probably heard someone swear and use the Lord's name. This breaks one of the Lord's commands. Other people use the Lord's name when they are angry, and this is also blasphemous. It's also possible to hurt people using the Lord's name. Unfortunately, there are people who masquerade as people of God but who bring harm in His name. When you speak the Lord's name, respect His power and authority, and do not cause harm to others.

Activity: Think of ways you can use the Lord's name to bring happiness and love to others.

February 3, 2013: Holy Is the Day of Worship
Exodus 20:8-11

"Remember the Sabbath day by keeping it holy." (Exod. 20:8, NIV).

In Genesis, we learn that God created the world in six days. On the seventh day, He rested. "'Therefore the LORD blessed the Sabbath day and made it holy'" (v. 11, NIV). The seventh day is meant to be a day of rest for God's people. After working for six days—just as God did creating the world—God's people are expected to rest. On this day of rest, the Lord should be worshiped, praised, and thanked for all He has given.

How do you spend your Sabbath day? Do you run around all day, trying to accomplish a long list of tasks? Do you begrudge having to get out of bed, get dressed, and go to church? Or do you find church to be an enjoyable place where you can recharge your batteries as you worship?

Worship isn't meant to be a chore. It's meant to be a celebration of God's love and faithfulness. If you find yourself dreading the Sabbath day or unable to even keep it holy for God, then it's time to figure out what's holding you back from obeying God. Everyone needs rest. Everyone also needs to respect God and give Him praise for His wonderful blessings. The Sabbath day is meant to be an occasion when we can spend time with God.

Activity: Write down how you've spent your last month of Sabbath days. How much of your time is spent with God?

February 10, 2013: Honor Your Parents
Exodus 20:12

"Honor your father and your mother, so that you may live long in the land the LORD your God is giving you." (Exod. 20:12, NIV)

The word *honor* means to show respect for someone or something. God tells the Israelites to honor their fathers and mothers. This is also a command for us. How do you show honor and respect? What qualities do you think merit honor? Do you think you should have to honor your parents if they're not honorable people?

In a perfect world, all mothers and fathers would be honorable. They would be worthy of admiration. Unfortunately, we are not all born to parents who are respectable. One thing to note about God's command: He does not tell us to honor our fathers and mothers if they are honorable. He says we must honor them; that's it. There's no way to make excuses about this command. Regardless of how our parents choose to live their lives, we must honor them. This doesn't mean we have to spend generous amounts of time with them. It doesn't require us to ever even visit them. God simply states that we must honor them. This might not be an easy task, but nowhere in the Bible does it state that following God and His commands is going to be the easy way of living. He has given all of us the strength to obey Him.

Activity: List people in your life who are honorable. How are you like them? How are you different?

February 17, 2013: Honor and Respect Life
Exodus 20:13

"You shall not murder." (Exod. 20:13, NIV)

More than twelve thousand people were murdered last year in the United States. Given that more than 311 million people live in the

United States, the number of murders might sound incredibly low—a mere four percent of the population. But according to God's Law, even one murder is one more than should ever occur.

We have learned the importance of respecting and honoring our parents. Today's devotional will teach us the importance of honoring and respecting life—all life. All humanity must value life. Life is fleeting and precious and changes from moment to moment. We do not have the right to end someone else's life. God is our Creator, and He is the only One who has the right to take the life of someone.

Murder might seem too extreme an action for you to ever take, but many people have thought the very same thing and found they were capable of extremes. How can we avoid murder? We can understand that murder is not the answer. It is, perhaps, a quick and easy fix to a difficult problem. However, murder creates problems of its own, and this is not the way to settle problems. God desires for us to share His Word with others, not take the lives of His creation.

Activity: How do you resolve your anger issues? How can you help someone who struggles with anger? Why is murder not the answer to our problems?

February 24, 2013: Adultery Is Not Okay
Exodus 20:14

"You shall not commit adultery." (Exod. 20:14, NIV)

The Bible is full of God's promises, and He has always and will always keep His Word. Marriage is a commitment a man and a woman make to each other. This commitment is a promise they vow they will not break. Adultery is one way sin can infiltrate a marriage and break apart this commitment.

When you yearn for someone other than your partner, you are committing adultery. You don't have to physically be with someone other than your spouse to commit adultery—it can happen with your eyes and with your thoughts. Fortunately, there are ways we can combat adultery. We can stop sinful thoughts before they corrupt our behavior and actions. We can keep our thoughts focused on God, helping to ensure that our thoughts, actions, reactions, and behavior are pure. Keeping yourself out of situations that might bring about sinful actions is also a good practice.

Activity: Keep a list of activities you enjoy participating in. Do these activities lead you away from God? Are there people in your life who keep you from fully committing to God?

March 3, 2013: Do Not Steal
Exodus 20:15

"You shall not steal." (Exod. 20:15, NIV)

As we keep discussing the Ten Commandments, we continue through the section of the Law which helps us to understand how we should treat ourselves and each other. Many of God's Laws are meant to protect us from harming ourselves and others. While some sins are blatantly harmful—like murder—others may seem more mundane. However, even a "mundane" sin can greatly affect your life and the lives of others.

You might desire something you can't afford. Most of us have felt that way, but feeling that way and acting sinfully upon that desire are two separate problems. We do not have the right to take what is not ours. God says so in today's commandment. Acquiring material possessions will not make us whole; it will not fulfill us. Only God can fulfill our needs.

Activity: Why do you think people have the desire to rate sins, saying this sin is better or worse than that sin? How do you feel about rating sins?

March 10, 2013: Do Not Speak Falsely
Exodus 20:16

"You shall not give false testimony against your neighbor." (Exod. 20:16, NIV)

If you say the words *false testimony* today, people will assume you are speaking about the deliberate and willful giving of false, misleading, or incomplete testimony under oath during a court proceeding. God commands the Israelites not to give false testimony against each other. He is referring to legal proceedings also, but He is also referring to lies told outside of the courtroom.

God's people are not to willfully charge people with false accusation or swear to these false accusations in order to hurt or damage one's life or livelihood. They are also not to privately whisper lies, slander, or harmful gossip about someone, thus soiling someone's character with insinuations and evil suggestions. Lies can greatly damage someone's life, job, marriage, and future. Lies ruin people's reputations, which can hurt many others in the process.

Activity: Why are lies hurtful? How can you avoid situations where you feel the need to lie?

March 17, 2013: Do Not Covet
Exodus 20:17

"You shall not covet your neighbor's house. You shall not covet your neighbor's wife, or his manservant or maidservant, his ox or donkey, or anything that belongs to your neighbor." (Exod. 20:17, NIV)

When you hear the word *covet*, what comes to your mind? Do you immediately think of today's commandment? What does it mean to covet? A simple dictionary definition explains that coveting means desiring to have that which belongs to another, even to the point of envy.

Envy is not one of humanity's admirable emotions, but it is a very normal one that we all experience during our lifetime. God tells His people not to covet their neighbor's belongings, not even their donkeys. It would be impossible for everyone to be on the same financial level as everyone else. This means there will be people in your life who seem to have it all—money, houses, clothing, jobs, etc. As God's children, we should not desire to have what our neighbors have.

Activity: Write down all the blessings in your life. Read through the list, and thank God for each one.

March 24, 2013: The Greatest Commandment
Mark 12:28-31

"The second is this: 'Love your neighbor as yourself.' There is no commandment greater than these." (Mark 12:31, NIV)

During a discussion with a teacher of the Law, Jesus is asked which commandment is the most important. Jesus tells the teacher that loving the Lord is the most important, but there is a second one: loving "'your neighbor as yourself'" (v. 31, NIV).

This commandment can bring into question a few ideas. How well do you love yourself? Are you good to yourself? Do you take care of yourself because your body is a temple of the Lord? Or are you hard on yourself? You are God's creation, and He loves you and desires that you take care of your temple. Second, are you good to others? Do you treat people as you would like to be treated? You are the representation of Christ in the world. Think about what people see when they see you. Are you a good example or do you leave people questioning what kind of person Jesus must have been?

Activity: How do you treat the temple of the Lord? Do you tak care of your body or do you neglect yourself? Rate yourself on a scale of 1-10 on how you treat others. Ask someone else to rate your treatment of others. How are the ratings different?

March 31, 2013: Love the Lord with All Your Heart
Mark 12:32-34

"To love him with all your heart, with all your understanding and with all your strength, and to love your neighbor as yourself is more important than all burnt offerings and sacrifices." (Mark 12:33, NIV)

If you were to name the one whom you love the most, who would be at the top of your list? How much do you love this person? Do you love him or her with all your heart or do you love depending on what kind of day you're having? Jesus said that the most important commandment was to love God with all one's heart, understanding, and strength. Jesus called for an all-consuming type of love, and this is the kind of love God wants from His children. He wants us to give Him all we have and keep giving more.

Activity: How do you think God loves you? Is His love all-consuming, forgiving, merciful, or patient? How do you love God? How much time do you give Him during the day?

Second Quarter 2013

AREA:
The Sermon on the Mount/Sermon on the Plain

QUARTERLY THEME:
God's Rules for Purposeful Living

LESSONS FOR APRIL—JUNE

April 7, 2013: Blessed Are the Poor in Spirit
Matthew 5:3

"Blessed are the poor in spirit, for theirs is the kingdom of heaven." (Matt. 5:3, NIV)

Today's lesson comes from Jesus' Sermon on the Mount, more specifically from the section we call "The Beatitudes." Jesus explains who will be blessed in God's kingdom. When Jesus speaks of the "poor in spirit," He does not mean those who are poor in respect to temporal possessions.

To be poor in spirit means you are humble, and you do not have an inflated opinion of yourself. You understand that you are a sinner, and you have no righteousness of your own. You know that you are saved only because God is full of grace and mercy. You follow God's Law, and you are a willing follower. You will go where He leads, and you will accept the burdens placed on your shoulders. You don't feel you deserve favor from Him, but you accept it and thank Him for His blessings and love. You are not proud or vain, and you are not full of selfish ambition. That is what it means to be poor in spirit.

What is your opinion of yourself? Do you act as though you're better than everyone else? Do you think you're so righteous you can judge others? Jesus says the humble will be blessed.

Activity: Write down how you view yourself. Are you confident or arrogant? Are you humble before the Lord or do you expect Him to bless you?

April 14, 2013: God Will Comfort Those Who Mourn Matthew 5:4

"Blessed are those who mourn, for they will be comforted." (Matt. 5:4, NIV)

By this point in your life, you have mourned something or someone—the breakup of a relationship, a death, a disappointment, etc. Jesus tells His listeners that those who mourn will be comforted. This statement alone is comforting. You can know that even when you are despairing and questioning your pain God will give you comfort.

Not only do you mourn situations that bring you pain, but you will also mourn sin and the results of sin. Sin is always working against you, and it will continually try to bring you grief. Sin can take root in your heart if you let it, and these roots will poison your heart with unbelief. You might mourn the sin that surrounds you and infects the people you love or other people in the world. It's easy to see the wickedness of the world and mourn. Sin destroys the earth, and it destroys God's people.

However, Jesus tells you that those who mourn will be comforted. Yes, sin is rampant, but there will be comfort for those who put their trust in God. God is stronger than sin, and He can give you strength to persevere during times of trouble. Remember that during these hardships, God is always with you—less than a breath away—giving you comfort and love.

Activity: What brings you comfort? Have you ever felt God's comfort during a difficult situation?

April 21, 2013: The Meek Shall Be Rewarded Matthew 5:5

"Blessed are the meek, for they will inherit the earth." (Matt. 5:5, NIV)

When you hear the word *meek*, does a negative connotation of the word pop into your head? Often, people think meekness is a less-than-desirable trait. But this is not the original connotation of the word. People wrongly assume that anyone who is meek is probably a pushover and can be easily manipulated.

In contrast to that impression, those who are meek are generally not easily provoked to anger. They patiently bear what life hands them with heads held high and mouths that are not prone to complaining. Meek people often deal with injuries and insults without retaliation. They are courteous and treat others fairly and kindly. They do not have arrogant opinions of themselves. They think the best of others, and they are not envious of the gifts and blessings others receive.

Because those who are meek are not arrogant, they take instruction and admonishment easily. In their private times, they willingly submit to God. They are thankful for God's mercy and grace, and they understand they would be nothing without God.

Contrary to what others may believe, meekness is commendable. Jesus tells the crowd that those who are meek will inherit God's kingdom. So the next time someone calls you meek, say thank you.

Activity: Take a look at the people in your life. Does anyone have meekness as a characteristic? Study how he or she lives his or her life. Would anyone call you meek?

April 28, 2013: Seeking Righteousness Pays Off
Matthew 5:6

"Blessed are those who hunger and thirst for righteousness, for they will be filled." (Matt. 5:6, NIV)

When you think of hunger and thirst, do you think of your favorite food or drink? What do you hunger for? A natural desire of our bodies is to seek to be filled with nourishment. You need food and drink to survive. Your body will warn you when it needs to be filled. Because the body is an earth-bound creation, hunger and thirst can only be physically satisfied with food or drink. Heavenly things cannot satisfy the natural cravings of the body's need for physical nourishment.

Likewise, the physical world cannot fulfill the needs of your spirit. Your soul depends on the nourishment given to you by God.

Earthly things cannot support the soul. When your soul is awakened to the desire for God, you hunger and thirst for God's righteousness. Nothing can satisfy your soul's desire except for God. You will only receive satisfaction when you are fed by the Living Bread and the Living Water—Jesus.

Jesus tells us that those who hunger for His righteousness will be filled. He will not leave us wanting; He will fill us with His love, grace, and mercy. Long after our earthly lives are over, we will continue to be filled with God's righteousness.

Activity: How do you satisfy your spiritual hunger and thirst? How does it feel to be filled with God's love?

May 5, 2013: Give Mercy, Get Mercy
Matthew 5:7

"Blessed are the merciful, for they will be shown mercy." (Matt. 5:7, NIV)

Mercy is a word you hear often, but you might not completely understand what it means. We hear *mercy* a lot in regard to the legal system. When someone is accused of a crime, this person might ask for others "to show mercy." Mercy is treating others with compassion and having a disposition to be kind and forgiving. Jesus says that those who show mercy will receive mercy from Him.

There are many ways you can show mercy to others. You can show compassion to those who are poor, needy, or unhappy. Showing compassion might mean you sympathize with their outward circumstances, but you can also give to them instead of only sharing expressions of concern and pity. You can communicate with them using a cheerful demeanor, showing affection and gentleness.

You can also show mercy to others by sharing the Word of God with them. You can offer good counsel and advice. You can direct them away from sin, pray for them, forgive any harm they have done to you in ignorance, and comfort them with the love of God. To show mercy is to imitate God. He shows us mercy for all of our faults, and you should follow His example.

Activity: What makes someone merciful? Are you merciful? Has anyone ever shown you mercy?

May 12, 2013: Do You Want to See God?
Matthew 5:8

"Blessed are the pure in heart, for they will see God." (Matt. 5:8, NIV)

What does it mean to be pure? Jesus tells His listeners that the pure in heart will see God. In Jesus' day, many Pharisees emphasized outward purity. Their conversations focused on what it meant to be righteous before others, but inside, they were full of impurities. They spoke of pure notions and actions, but their hearts were impure. They were all talk. They did not know what it means to be truly righteous.

Because we are infected with sin, humans are naturally unclean. We do not have the ability to make ourselves clean and wipe away the stains of sin. We cannot free ourselves from the bonds of sin—only Christ can free us from our bondage. We are made clean by His sacrifice. We have been forgiven, and our imperfect hearts can be made pure.

However, staying pure isn't always easy. Sin is ready to tempt you away from God's righteousness. But God has given you the strength to abstain from sin. You can keep your heart pure and focused on God. Once your heart has tasted the purity given to you by God, you will desire more. You will want to fill your life, words, and heart with this purity.

Activity: What does purity mean to you? Do you believe God has given you the strength to say no to sin? What would it be like for you to see God?

May 19, 2013: Make Peace, Not War
Matthew 5:9

"Blessed are the peacemakers, for they will be called sons of God." (Matt. 5:9, NIV)

Arguments are a part of life. You won't always agree with everyone you meet. But there is a difference in debating others on a topic and being someone who instigates arguments. Jesus tells the crowd that the peacemakers are blessed and will be recognized as the children of God.

Peacemakers are important. You might have experienced a situation where you could not and would not see eye-to-eye with the other person involved in the confrontation. A peacemaker is necessary to smooth things over, to help you both find a good compromise, and to stop the argument from getting out of hand.

Peacemakers are those who have peaceful dispositions. For the most part, they live peaceably with all people, finding no need to incite anger in those around them. Peacemakers are often ready and willing to be of service in disagreeable circumstances. They serve to make peace between all people and between Christians also. Just because people are Christians doesn't exclude them from heated arguments that become too large to control.

Children of God seek to work together fairly, efficiently, and in a unified manner. They do not want division in the Church, so they work to bring people together, even people with differences. Peacemakers help to heal the world instead of dividing it.

Activity: Why do you think peacemakers are important? Do you know any peacemakers? How have they made the world a better place?

May 26, 2013: Persecuted but Not Forgotten
Matthew 5:10

"Blessed are those who are persecuted because of righteousness, for theirs is the kingdom of heaven." (Matt. 5:10, NIV)

Jesus tells His listeners that those who are persecuted will receive the kingdom of heaven. By persecution, He did not mean those who have committed crimes and are on trial, such as murderers, thieves, and evildoers. Rather, Jesus meant those who are persecuted because they are His followers and are following the path of righteousness. These persecuted followers are hated because of their righteousness and devotion to God. By being Christians, they are separated from the world, and they even admit they do not belong to the world.

By setting yourself apart from the world, you are admitting that you follow a higher calling. This truth can and will upset those who feel you are condemning them and calling them wicked. Many will become angry with you and strike out against you. Sometimes, simply saying that you follow Christ will turn people against you. You will be a target for their ridicule and mockery. By following Christ, you expose yourself to the taunts, anger, and persecution of others, but you must embrace your calling. You must continue to preach and teach the Word because God is on your side, and He will bless you for your perseverance and constant devotion to Him.

Activity: Have you ever been persecuted for your beliefs? How did you respond? How did it change your life? Why is persecution by those we love so much more painful than the persecution of strangers?

June 2, 2013: Blessed for Believing
Matthew 5:11-12

"Blessed are you when people insult you, persecute you and falsely say all kinds of evil against you because of me." (Matt. 5:11, NIV)

Today's verses are a continuation of last week's discussion concerning persecution. Jesus' words were most likely directed at His disciples. He informs them that they will not be exempt from persecution, and He wants to fortify them against these attacks. In the *King James Version*, the word *insult* is translated revile. A simple dictionary definition of revile is "to assail with abusive language." This is definitely a form of persecution that can be difficult to handle.

As a Christian, you subject yourself to the insults thrown at you by those who choose not to follow Christ's path. People will say all manner of evil against you, soiling your name—and, perhaps, your reputation—as they seek to disgrace and embarrass you. This is one of Satan's ways of chipping away at your resolve. He hopes to bring you to the point where you say, "This is too difficult. I give up." But because Jesus has already warned you of such happenings, you can be ready for what is to come. You can prepare your heart for hardships.

Jesus tells you to rejoice and be glad during your hardships because He will greatly bless you in the Kingdom that is to come. He offers His comfort, reminding you that you are not alone in your sufferings. Remember that even the prophets, who came before you, suffered in the same way.

Activity: Pray for those who are persecuted in your country and throughout the world.

June 9, 2013: Be Salty
Matthew 5:13

"You are the salt of the earth. But if the salt loses its saltiness, how can it be made salty again? It is no longer good for anything, except to be thrown out and trampled by men." (Matt. 5:13, NIV)

Jesus says you are the salt of the earth, but what does He mean? Salt is a seasoning, but it's also a preservative. A preservative is a substance added to food in order to keep it from spoiling. People have used salt as a preservative for thousands of years.

When Jesus compares you to salt, He means two things. First, Jesus means for you to understand that you are to make the world a better place, just as salt makes food taste better. You can change the world simply by being a part of it. You can spread God's love to others and enhance their lives. Have you ever put too much salt on your food? What happened to the food? Were you able to eat it? You must remember that too much salt can ruin the taste of food, and You must not be overbearing when you are sharing God's love. Just the right amount of salt must be added in order to be effective. Jesus also means that because you are the salt of the earth you can help preserve the world from spoiling caused by sin.

Activity: How can you be the salt of the earth without being abrasive or suffocating? How can you spread the Word in a way that enhances the lives of others?

June 16, 2013: A Beacon of Light
Matthew 5:14

"You are the light of the world. A city on a hill cannot be hidden." (Matt. 5:14, NIV)

Jesus uses another comparison in verse fourteen. He says, "You are the light of the world" (v. 14, NIV). Anytime there is light in a dark room, the darkness must leave. Light and darkness cannot exist in the same space. This is also true in the life of a believer. Your heart must be filled with the light of Jesus, and you are meant to shine your light to everyone in the world. When you are filled with the love and truth of Jesus, you cannot hide your faith. You are like "a city on a hill [that] cannot be hidden" (ibid.). Everyone will know whom you serve.

When you know and love Jesus, you should not hide His love from others. Jesus says people do not light a lamp and then hide it under a bowl. When you light a lamp, you place it out so that the light can shine and others can see. Everyone around benefits from the light. The same happens when you shine the light of Jesus onto others around you. People will benefit from the truth, and they can find their way to Jesus.

You should let your light shine. You should not hide the light that Jesus has put into your heart. Why do some people hide the light of Jesus? Maybe they are afraid. Maybe they want to fit in with others, and loving Jesus isn't the popular decision. You should always be willing and ready to shine your light to anyone and everyone.

Activity: Why is it important to let your light shine? Think about the words to the song, "This Little Light of Mine." How do you shine your light?

June 23, 2013: Practice and Teach Others
Matthew 5:19

"Anyone who breaks one of the least of these commandments and teaches others to do the same will be called least in the kingdom of heaven, but whoever practices and teaches these commands will be called great in the kingdom of heaven." (Matt. 5:19, NIV)

In today's verses, Jesus speaks about those who make divisions between sins. The Pharisees had a habit of dividing the laws according to their opinions of lesser laws and greater laws. They said one could violate a lesser law and be guilty of a trivial offense only. Christ teaches the people that those who make this distinction, or teach that any laws of God might be broken with exemption from punishment, will be called "least." Those who hold the Law in high regard and respect the laws of God will be called great in God's kingdom.

Some people continue to rate sins according to their opinions of which sin is worse than another. Jesus tells the people there is no distinction between sins (or those who have made some laws more important than others). A sin is still a sin, and a law of God is still a law of God. One cannot break a law and say, "This is only a small law. At least I didn't kill anyone." Jesus says that such people will not be highly regarded.

How do you view God's laws? Do you make divisions and choose which laws are important to you? All of God's laws are important. He expects us to respect Him and respect His Word.

Activity: Why do people continue to try and rate laws and sins from greatest to least importance? How can you stop yourself from this bad habit? How can you place importance on all of God's laws?

June 30, 2013: Blessed for Prioritizing
Matthew 6:33

"But seek first his kingdom and his righteousness, and all these things will be given to you as well." (Matt. 6:33, NIV)

You probably have a to-do list. What's at the top? Do you run around through most of your week only to find your list grows longer? You have priorities, and you have tasks that need to be accomplished. We all do. God knows that you need to get jobs done in order to have a peaceful and functioning life, but God also wants to be a priority in your life—the top priority.

In the middle of your chaotic week, stop and speak to the Lord. Talk to Him; tell Him how you're feeling, what you're thankful for, and what you're nervous or excited about. Seek Him in the morning when you rise. Seek Him all throughout the day. He wants to hear from you.

Jesus tells His listeners that if they seek the kingdom of heaven, all they need will be fulfilled. God can fulfill all of our needs. He wants to bless us, but we must seek Him before everything and everyone else.

Activity: Make a list of priorities. Rework the list to put God's name all throughout your day. Before long, you won't need a list to remind you to seek God all day long.

Third Quarter 2013

AREA:
The Sermon on the Mount/Sermon on the Plain

QUARTERLY THEME:
Following Jesus' Instructions

LESSONS FOR JULY—SEPTEMBER

July 7, 2013: Control Your Anger
Matthew 5:21-26

"But I tell you that anyone who is angry with his brother will be subject to judgment." (Matt. 5:22, NIV)

You know it's wrong to murder because it breaks one of the Ten Commandments. Those who murder have allowed anger to overcome them, and they have acted upon these emotions. During His Sermon on the Mount, Jesus explains that even those who are angry with another will be subject to judgment.

Have you ever been angry with someone? Did you feel your anger was warranted or justified? In this passage, Jesus warns about the dangers of anger turning to hatred and bitterness. Jesus says that you cannot bring your gifts to the altar of God if you have allowed bitterness to take root in your heart. Bitterness can poison your heart. It can start as a small seed and grow until it consumes you. How can you worship God when your heart is poisoned? You can't. Your thoughts and emotions are tangled around the sin of hatred. You must have a clean heart before you can truly worship.

Jesus says to go and reconcile to the person. After you have reconciled, then you can offer your gifts to God on the altar. This route of forgiveness and reconciliation is needed in order for you to truly praise God. Don't let your anger control you. Take control of it.

Activity: How often do you find yourself angry with others? Have you ever tried to reconcile with someone? How can you keep your anger under control?

July 14, 2013: Do Not Lust
Matthew 5:27-30

"You have heard that it was said, 'Do not commit adultery.'" (Matt. 5:27, NIV)

During the first quarter of this devotional, you learned about the commandment that commands you not to commit adultery. You learned that you don't have to commit physical acts in order to commit adultery. Jesus tells His listeners, "'Anyone who looks at a woman lustfully has already committed adultery with her in his heart'" (v. 28, NIV). Jesus says that if your right eye is the reason for your sin, then you should "'gouge it out and throw it away'" (v. 29, NIV). This might sound a little drastic, so let's put it in modern terms.

Jesus wants to express the extreme nature of this sin. What lengths would you go to in order to stop yourself from sinning? Do you look at sin as something mildly dangerous? Do you understand that sin can destroy your life and the lives of others involved? Jesus says it's better to lose an eye than to allow the entire body to be destroyed. You must do whatever it takes to keep yourself out of sinful situations. Even though Jesus isn't actually asking you to gouge out your eyes, He wants you to understand that avoiding sin is serious and you should go to extremes to keep yourself pure. You cannot risk the state of your soul in order to dabble in sin. Take your purity seriously because Jesus does.

Activity: How can you keep yourself out of sinful environments? Have you ever had to go to extremes to remove yourself from sin's path of destruction? Have you ever had to help someone out of a sinful situation?

July 21, 2013: Honor Your Vows
Matthew 5:31-32

"It has been said, 'Anyone who divorces his wife must give her a certificate of divorce.'" (Matt. 5:31, NIV)

Marriage is a commitment made between a man and a woman. There are many wonderful parts of marriage and sharing lives together, but marriage isn't always easy. No one makes the promise that marriage will be problem-free. What two people promise is to help each other through difficult times and good times. There are promises made to support each other when life is full of fun and adventure, when money is tight, when the pantry is bare, when everything is smooth sailing, and when health ebbs and flows.

Honoring your wedding vows takes work sometimes, while others times it might be as easy as breathing. Regardless of the ease you do or do not experience, honoring your vows—whether they are marital or otherwise—is very important to God. God never loosely makes His promises to us, and He expects us to take our commitments seriously, too.

Just as you must cultivate and nourish your soul by spending time with God, you should also make sure you take care of your marital relationship. All relationships need to be tended to in order to keep them healthy. Don't neglect your relationship with God, and don't neglect the vows you have made.

Activity: Make a list of promises you have made. How many have you kept? List ways you can keep your relationships healthy and thriving.

July 28, 2013: Answer Yes or No
Matthew 5:33-37

"Simply let your 'Yes' be 'Yes,' and your 'No,' 'No'; anything beyond this comes from the evil one." (Matt. 5:37, NIV)

When you give someone your word, it's important to keep it. People depend on you to follow through with what actions or tasks you say you're going to perform. When you break your word, your promise, or an oath, there are people—other than yourself—who are affected. God made many promises in the Bible, and He has kept every one. He is the example to follow when it comes to following through with your word.

Today's verses say to not swear (or make oaths) at all. During the time of this passage, people often swore by the king's throne, by the names of cities, or by God's name, which was blasphemous. Jesus tells the people this type of swearing and trying to ensure the seriousness of one's oath is wrong. While they should keep their oaths to the Lord, they should not swear by anything else—not by the king's throne, by false gods, or by the Lord's name.

When you agree to do something, you should let your yes be yes and your no be no. Do not agree to do tasks that you cannot or do not plan to perform. Allow people to trust your word and prove you are a dependable person.

Activity: Do you stick to your word? Do you agree to help people and then neglect to keep your promises to them? How can you let your yes mean yes and your no mean no?

August 4, 2013: Do Not Trade Evil for Evil
Matthew 5:38-42

"But I tell you, Do not resist an evil person. If someone strikes you on the right cheek, turn to him the other also." (Matt. 5:39, NIV)

The "eye for an eye" command is found in Exodus 21:24, Leviticus 24:20, and Deuteronomy 19:21. This command was used as a rule to regulate the decisions of judges. But God did not intend this command to be used in private conduct. Many people consider this rule as justification to inflict the same injury on someone else who has done an injury to them. Jesus declares this law has no reference to private revenge.

Jesus says that if someone strikes you, you are to turn the other cheek. How often have you wanted to retaliate against someone who has done you harm? This is not Jesus' way. He says if someone wants your tunic, give him your cloak as well. We are not to enact revenge. In fact, Moses told the Israelites these words about God: "'It is mine to avenge; I will repay'" (Deut. 32:35, NIV). Even though you've been hurt by others, you must not willfully hurt them in return. Leave vengeance to God.

Activity: How do you feel about revenge? Do you think it's ever justified? How can you hand over your anger to God and turn the other cheek?

August 11, 2013: Love Your Enemy
Matthew 5:43-48

"But I tell you: Love your enemies and pray for those who persecute you." (Matt. 5:44, NIV)

The Jews knew they should love their neighbors, but their definition of neighbors was small and confined to only those of the Jewish race. The believed everyone else was their enemy. Jesus tells the listeners today that their neighbors are not simply people of their race, people who live next door, or people they see in the temple. Their neighbors include everyone in the whole world. All of God's children are our neighbors.

Who do you think is your neighbor? Are your neighbors the people in your community? Do you believe those outside of your church, neighborhood, or race are your enemies? Even though your neighbors should include everyone, not everyone will be kind to you. Jesus tells you to "'pray for those who persecute you'" (v. 44, NIV). Jesus loves all people, even those who are wicked and turn away from Him. It isn't an easy task to love those who insult you, but Jesus says that loving those who love you is easy. Even pagans love those who love them. Being His follower isn't easy, and He will challenge you to step outside your comfort zone. Move outside the box. Love and pray for those who hurt you. Reach out to those who you may not have considered to be your neighbors. Share the Word of God.

Activity: Make a list of who you believed your neighbors were before this lesson. Who do you believe your neighbors are now? Do you move out of your comfort zone in order to share the Word?

August 18, 2013: Practice the Golden Rule
Luke 6:31

"Do to others as you would have them do to you." (Luke 6:31, NIV)

Treating others the way we want to be treated can be an incredibly easy task. You might send people cards, telling them how special they are. You might meet with friends once a week and discuss your lives in order to keep relationships healthy. You might bake or cook for those who are in need. You might even volunteer your time to those who are in need.

But how do you treat those who mistreat you? Do you turn the other cheek or do you pray for them? This can be problematic when dealing with people who hurt you, don't appreciate what you do or how you act, or simply don't care about you at all. People can be hurtful, but how do you treat them? Do you still reach out to them and treat them the way you would hope to be treated? This can be a difficult lesson to learn. But if you follow this rule, you are following the heart of Jesus, and you are allowing your heart and spirit to grow and strengthen.

Activity: How important do you believe the Golden Rule is? Do you follow this rule? Would you share this rule with others?

August 25, 2013: Judge Not
Luke 6:37

"Do not judge, and you will not be judged. Do not condemn, and you will not be condemned. Forgive, and you will be forgiven (Luke 6:37, NIV)

Judging is something that comes naturally to most of us. Is this restaurant better than the other one? Is this car more comfortable than that one? Do you like your English professor better than your economics professor? You judge all sorts of things every day. It's easy to become ensnared in the web of judgment. Jesus tells you, "'Do not judge, and you will not be judged'" (v. 37, NIV). If we were to be judged as harshly as we judge others, it would definitely change our perspective.

If you were completely honest, you'd probably say you didn't like people to judge you. You don't want to be singled out and picked apart. But it's easy to forget how you'd feel if the shoe were on the foot. You might not even realize how often you judge others until you start imagining all those people judging you. Jesus tells you not to condemn others. Don't pretend you have the power to judge people and send them to hell for their sins. This is not your job, and you certainly don't have the power to do any such condemning. Instead of judging others, love them, forgive them, and share God's grace with them.

Activity: How can you stop yourself from judging others? How can you put yourself in their shoes before you jump to conclusions, condemn them, or separate yourself from them? Why is it important to forgive others?

September 1, 2013: Straighten Out Yourself First
Luke 6:41-42

"How can you say to your brother, 'Brother, let me take the speck out of your eye,' when you yourself fail to see the plank in your own eye? You hypocrite, first take the plank out of your eye, and then you will see clearly to remove the speck from your brother's eye." (Luke 6:42, NIV)

Sometimes, it's easy to judge others and overlook everything you might be doing, where you are lacking, and the areas of your life that need shoring up. Jesus asks the people, "'Why do you look at the speck of sawdust in your brother's eye and pay no attention to the plank in your own eye?'" (v. 41, NIV). Perhaps you think your sins are not as significant as the sins of others. Perhaps you have begun to rate sins, and you think your wrongdoings pale in comparison to your neighbor's much larger sins. A sin is still a sin, and, unfortunately, all humans are sinners. At some point in your life, you have sinned. You are in need of forgiveness just as much as your neighbor is in need of it.

Activity: Why do you think we like to pretend our lives are cleaner and freer of sin than the lives of others? How can you be a better friend to those who are in need of guidance?

September 8, 2013: Build Your Life on the Rock
Luke 6:46-49

"He is like a man building a house, who dug down deep and laid the foundation on rock. When a flood came, the torrent struck that house but could not shake it, because it was well built." (Luke 6:48, NIV)

Jesus is your Cornerstone. Without Him, you cannot build a solid foundation. He is the Rock who brings all parts of your life together, connects all parts of you, and makes you strong enough to withstand life's trials. Without Jesus, your life would crumble like a house built of sand along the shore.

However, if you listen to Jesus' words and you plant them in your heart to grow, you are like a woman who has dug down deep, laid a solid foundation, and built a strong house. When the waves rush your house, your house will not be shaken because your house is well-built. You will be able to withstand the trials of life because you put Jesus' words into practice, and He lives within your heart, giving your strength and comfort.

Activity: Have you laid a solid foundation? Have you put Jesus' words into practice? When trials come your way, are you shaken or do you stand firmly with Jesus as your foundation?

September 15, 2013: Acts of Righteousness
Matthew 6:1-8

"Be careful not to do your 'acts of righteousness' before men, to be seen by them. If you do, you will have no reward from your Father in heaven." (Matt. 6:1, NIV)

It is one thing to discuss what you have done during your missions or Kingdom building activities so that others can know of what can be done, what is being done, and how they can help. It is another thing to brag to others because you want them to see how much you are doing to help others. God sees what you do, and He will reward you, so there is no need to boast about your deeds to others. Acts of service are meant to bring others to Christ, help those who are in need, and strengthen your heart for God.

Jesus warns you not to "'do your "acts of righteousness" before men, to be seen by them'" (v. 1, NIV). As simple and obvious as this sounds, we all sometimes fall victim to this desire. We want to be noticed and seen by others. We like to hear we have done a job well, but Jesus explains that God knows exactly what we do. When He sees us helping His children, He is proud of us.

Activity: How can you make sure your acts of righteousness are not done simply to please people?

September 22, 2013: The Model Prayer
Luke 6:9-15

"This, then, is how you should pray: 'Our Father in heaven, hallowed be your name.'" (Matt. 6:9, NIV)

Some of the people listening to Jesus during the Sermon on the Mount did not know exactly how to pray. Jesus tells them, "'This, then, is how you should pray'" (v. 9, NIV).

First, you should address the Lord, whose name is holy and revered. Jesus says you should acknowledge that God's kingdom is coming and you wish to follow His will on earth just as it is followed in heaven. Pray that God will supply you with the daily nourishment that you need—both physically and spiritually.

Then, pray that God will forgive your sins just as you strive to forgive those who have sinned against you. If you forgive those who have hurt you, then God will also forgive you. However, if you do not forgive others, you will not be forgiven.

Finally, pray that God will keep you from temptation, so that you do not fall prey to sins. Pray that God will deliver you from the devil, so that your heart will always belong to God.

Activity: How do you pray? The Lord's Prayer is a good reference for how you should pray on a daily basis. Read the Lord's Prayer aloud. Read it slowly and really think about each phrase.

September 29, 2013: Treasures in Heaven
Matthew 6:19-21

"But store up for yourselves treasures in heaven, where moth and rust do not destroy, and where thieves do not break in and steal." (Matt. 6: 20, NIV)

You probably have a bank account. You might even have a retirement fund. You use these services to store and safeguard your money and other financial holdings.

What do you store in your home—photo albums, family memorabilia, or keepsakes? You might even go to great lengths to keep your home safe with an alarm system or security lights. Your reasons for wanting to protect your money and your possessions are valid, but what are you doing to protect your eternal future?

Jesus tells His listeners not to store their treasures on earth because possessions will rust and decay. Possessions can be stolen. However, if you store up your treasures in heaven, they will be forever protected. Treasures in heaven will not be destroyed or stolen. Take stock of where your treasures are.

Activity: Make a list of your greatest possessions. Make a list of the ways you can store up your possessions in heaven.

Fourth Quarter 2013

AREA:
Rules for Living

QUARTERLY THEME:
Commands from Jesus from Matthew and Luke

LESSONS FOR OCTOBER—DECEMBER

October 6, 2013: Give to Others
Matthew 6:2-4

"So when you give to the needy, do not announce it with trumpets, as the hypocrites do in the synagogues and on the streets, to be honored by men. I tell you the truth, they have received their reward in full." (Matt. 6:2, NIV)

Many missions deal completely with those who are underprivileged, undernourished, and in need of daily necessities. Multiple Bible verses explain the importance of giving to those who are in need. In Luke, John the Baptist speaks to those who ask what should be done for the needy: "John answered, 'The man with two tunics should share with him who has none, and the one who has food should do the same'" (Luke 3:11, NIV). Later in Luke 6, Jesus says, "'Give, and it will be given to you. A good measure, pressed down, shaken together and running over, will be poured into your lap. For with the measure you use, it will be measured to you'" (v. 38, NIV).

Giving to the needy is an act of service, and just like the acts of service we discussed earlier, these acts are not meant to be done in public so everyone can see what you've done. You do not need to "'announce it with trumpets, as the hypocrites do in the synagogues and on the streets, to be honored by men'" (Matt. 6:2, NIV). Giving to others should be done without expecting fanfare. God will see what you have done, and you will be rewarded. There is no need for you to toot your own horn.

Activity: How can you help provide for the needy?

October 13, 2013: Acts for God
Matthew 6:16-18

"When you fast, do not look somber as the hypocrites do, for they disfigure their faces to show men they are fasting. I tell you the truth, they have received their reward in full." (Matt. 6:16, NIV)

There are many different ways you can give glory to God. There are also ways you can unplug from everyday life in order to spend time with God in silence. You can turn off all electronic devices for a set amount of time and commune with God, making sure you are not interrupted. You can visit a park and spend time outside, helping to clear your mind from the busy day-to-day hassles of life. You can also choose to fast. Often, people choose fasting as a means of turning their focus completely on God. They do not want to be distracted by even something as simple and commonplace as food. Many people fasted in the Bible as a way to draw closer to God.

You have learned the difference between performing your acts of service before people in order to be recognized and performing your acts in secret where only God knows what you are doing. The same is to be said of acts like fasting. Jesus says, "'But when you fast, put oil on your head and wash your face, so that it will not be obvious to men that you are fasting, but only to your Father, who is unseen; and your Father, who sees what is done in secret, will reward you'" (vv. 17-18, NIV).

Activity: Where do you go or what do you do when it's time to spend quiet time with God? How do you unplug from daily life?

October 20, 2013: You Cannot Serve Two Masters
Matthew 6:24

"No one can serve two masters. Either he will hate the one and love the other, or he will be devoted to the one and despise the other. You cannot serve both God and Money." (Matt. 6:24, NIV)

To be mastered means to be subjected to domination or subjugation. The Thirteenth Amendment abolished slavery in the United

States in 1865. With the passing of this amendment, involuntary servitude and slavery were outlawed. The ending of slavery was a giant step toward freedom. However, the ending of involuntary servitude forced upon people by others did not end the slavery in which we often still find ourselves.

Whatever masters you makes you its slave. Are you a slave to your job, to your partner, to your desire for possessions, wealth, or greener grass? Are you a Christian who has yoked herself to other slave masters, not necessarily other people? Jesus says you cannot serve two masters. You either serve Him or you serve something or someone else. He gives an example that you cannot serve both God and money, but there are many other parts of your life that can master you.

Jesus came and broke the yoke of slavery for you. He freed you of your sins. You do not have to be bound to slavery by people or possessions or desires. You are free, and Jesus will fill your heart so that your only desire will be serve Him—your one, true Master.

Activity: Have you allowed someone or something to master you? How can you start the process of freeing yourself or allowing Jesus to set you free?

October 27, 2013: Do Not Worry
Matthew 6:25

"Therefore I tell you, do not worry about your life, what you will eat or drink; or about your body, what you will wear. Is not life more important than food, and the body more important than clothes?" (Matt. 6:25, NIV)

Worrying is something you probably feel powerless to stop sometimes. There are many factors in your life that might cause you to worry, such as bills, your children, your aging parents, your job, or your purpose in life. There is a saying, "If you worry, why pray? If you pray, why worry?" You're not powerless to stop worrying when it starts. Jesus is always by your side, so why do you have any need to worry? He is in constant control of your ship.

Jesus tells the listening crowd, "'Do not worry about your life'" (v. 25, NIV). Jesus says to not concern yourself with your clothes, your body, or nourishment. He knows what you need, and He has everything you need in order to be provided for. So when worrying plagues you, stop and pray. Tell Jesus how you're feeling. Tell Him about your worries, and then let them go. Give your worries over to Jesus because He is taking care of you, and He will not lead you astray.

Activity: What worries you the most? How can you stop these worries as soon as they start?

November 3, 2013: More Than Sparrows
Matthew 6:26

"Look at the birds of the air; they do not sow or reap or store away in barns, and yet your heavenly Father feeds them. Are you not much more valuable than they?" (Matt. 6:26, NIV)

During the last devotional you learned why it is pointless to worry. If God is taking care of everything and He is the Captain of your ship, why do you have any need to worry? You don't. The birds don't worry about what they will eat. They don't spend their days reaping and sowing and storing seeds in barns. And, still, they have food to eat because God takes care of them. Jesus asks, "'Are you not much more valuable than they?'" (v. 26, NIV). If God can and does take care of the animals, wouldn't He take care of you because you are His greatest creation?

Life is full of trials, and it's easy to become consumed in what will happen in the future. You want to control your life and have everything in order just as you want it, but God has a greater plan for you. You cannot control everything. You must give the control over to God because you are more important to Him than the sparrows, yet He takes care of the sparrows, too. When you feel yourself slipping into control mode or worrying over what tomorrow will bring, remember the birds. Remember that God takes care of even the smallest creatures, and He will certainly take care of you.

Activity: Write down how you feel about letting go of control. How does it make you feel to know God has control of your life?

November 10, 2013: Trust God
Matthew 6:27-32

"Who of you by worrying can add a single hour to his life?" (Matt. 6:27, NIV)

Studies show that stress ages you faster than almost anything else. Jesus tells you that you will not add a single hour to your life by worrying. So why do you bother? Jesus continues to explain to His listeners that the lilies do not worry about what will happen to them: "'They do not labor or spin'" (v. 28, NIV). God has created a beautiful world. He has provided the lilies with splendor, so wouldn't He give you even more blessings? Wouldn't He create something even more wonderful for you?

Jesus warns that the pagans run around, worrying about what they will eat and drink. They do not have faith in God because they do not believe in Him. They do not know that God will provide for them if only they would believe and ask. You are not a pagan. You know that God will provide for you. You know His love is immense, and He will take care of you. So why do you worry? Why do you act like the pagans? Put your trust in God and know that He is worthy of your trust. God knows what you need, and He is already providing for you.

Activity: How can you work to eliminate stress from your life? How can you give your trust fully to God?

November 17, 2013: Ask the Lord
Matthew 7:7-11

"Ask and it will be given to you; seek and you will find; knock and the door will be opened to you. For everyone who asks receives; he who seeks finds; and to him who knocks, the door will be opened." (Matt. 6:7-8, NIV)

Prayer is important to God. When Jesus lived on earth, He took time to pray to God, which is a perfect example of how crucial communication with the Father is to our lives. Today's verses emphasize communication with God in earnestness, diligence, and perseverance. Jesus promises you that if you ask of Him, He will provide for you. If you seek Him with a spirit that is humble, sincere, and persevering, you will find Him. If you knock, the door will be opened for you. Just as beggars knock at doors in order to seek assistance and compassion, you knock at the door of mercy, asking God, in faith, for His assistance and grace. This seeking and knocking shows persistence and proves to God that you truly desire for Him to be a part of your life.

Have you ever played the childhood game Hide-and-Seek? Have you ever been the one who hid and waited for someone to find you? Imagine if no one ever found you. Imagine how lonely and forgotten you would feel. God waits for us to seek Him, and He promises that if we do seek Him, we will find Him. God isn't hiding from us, but like childhood seekers, we need to strike out in search of Him. He has so much to offer us.

Activity: How do you seek God? How often do you knock on the door?

November 24, 2013: The Narrow Way
Matthew 7:13-14

"Enter through the narrow gate. For wide is the gate and broad is the road that leads to destruction, and many enter through it. But small is the gate and narrow the road that leads to life, and only a few find it." (Matt. 7:13-14, NIV)

How easy is it to be led to sin? Can you turn the corner of your block and find something wicked to take part in? Can you sit around at work and fall victim to gossip, tossing in your opinions and assumed thoughts about others? Jesus says the road to destruction is broad and the gate is wide. This pathway can coax in many people because it's the easy way. There doesn't seem to be any obstacles on the road to destruction. There's plenty of room for everyone, but the end result is death and devastation.

Jesus says the path of the righteous can be entered at the "strait gate" (v. 13, KJV). The word *strait* has archaic meanings that better help us to understand Jesus' meaning than modern-day uses of *strait*. According to those older definitions of *strait*, the "strait gate" would have been narrow, tightly fitted, constricted, confining, and affording little space or room. This does not sound like an easy or comfortable gate to pass through. It might be tempting to choose the broad and wide path, and you can see why many people choose that way. But destruction and death are certainly not worth the temporary comforts of the broad road. Jesus says, "'Enter through the narrow gate'" because only that "'road leads to life'" (vv. 13, 14, NIV).

Activity: Pray that you will always strive to follow the path of righteousness. Although the broad way is tempting, it leads to death. Life can only be found by entering through the narrow gate.

December 1, 2013: Watch for the Fruit
Matthew 7:15-20

"Watch out for false prophets. They come to you in sheep's clothing, but inwardly they are ferocious wolves." (Matt. 7:15, NIV)

If people wore signs that described the inner workings of their spirits, false prophets or evildoers would be much easier to spot. You could avoid someone wearing a sign that read: False Teacher. Unfortunately, many evildoers and false teachers "'come to you in sheep's clothing, but inwardly they are ferocious wolves'" (v. 15, NIV). You might fall victim to these false teachers because they are charming, articulate, and magnetic. But Jesus says you can recognize them by the fruit they bear.

You bear fruit, too. If you fill your heart with the Word and live according to God's will, you will bear good fruit. It will be impossible for you to fill your Spirit with God and bear bad fruit. Bad teachers, on the other hand, are not filled with the Spirit, and the fruit they bear will be rotten. Jesus says, "'Every tree that does not bear good fruit is cut down and thrown into the fire,'" (v. 19, NIV). False teachers are easy to recognize by their fruit. They are normally consumed with pride, lust, the need for public recognition, and arrogance. True teachers of God do not give evidence of these things in their lives. They do the work of God because the Spirit fills their hearts.

Activity: Have you ever encountered a false teacher? What kind of fruit do you think you bear?

December 8, 2013: Secrets Shall Be Revealed
Luke 8:16-17

"No one lights a lamp and hides it in a jar or puts it under a bed. Instead, he puts it on a stand, so that those who come in can see the light." (Luke 8:16, NIV)

Christ tells His disciples that although the mysteries of the Kingdom are often spoken about using parables, they will not be understood by some people. Jesus often explains the meaning of the parables because He does not intend for the secrets of the Kingdom to always remain a secret. He oftentimes speaks to His disciples in private because He intends for them to continue spreading the Gospel long after He has left the earth.

You are the light of the world, and you should communicate with others because Jesus has shared many secrets with you. You know the Gospel, and you know the impact it can have on others. You have knowledge because you have the Bible and Jesus' teachings, and there are others who have neither. You are not meant to keep the Gospel a secret like a light hidden under a jar. You are meant to spread your light to others. Don't bottle up the Word of God in your heart and keep it for yourself. Share what you know with others. Shine the light of God into the lives of others.

Activity: How can you act like a light in the world? How can you share the Gospel?

December 15, 2013: Deny Yourself
Luke 9:23-25

Then he said to them all: "If anyone would come after me, he must deny himself and take up his cross daily and follow me." (Luke 9:23, NIV)

Have you ever wondered why bad things happen to good people? This seems to be a fairly common question asked among all people, not just Christians. Have you ever wondered that and then thought about Jesus' disciples? These men gave up their livelihoods, time with the families, and sometimes their reputations in order to follow Christ. Their lives were not easy, and they were more often than not extremely difficult lives. Many of Jesus' disciples were murdered for their beliefs. Looking at these men, you might say they are good men. You might not think they deserved to experience "bad things," but these men would likely tell you it was worth it. They understood they would be punished for their devotion to God and His Son.

Following Christ isn't going to be easy. You aren't going to be able to bypass difficult and painful situations simply because you follow Jesus. You are not exempt from hardships. All people—believers and non-believers alike—will experience difficulties. What makes you different from an unbeliever is that you trust in God. You ask Him for guidance. You will deny yourself and follow Him. And God will take care of you.

Activity: How can you take up your cross daily to follow Christ? What does self-denial mean to you?

December 22, 2013: Childlike Faith
Luke 9:48

Then he said to them, "Whoever welcomes this little child in my name welcomes me; and whoever welcomes me welcomes the one who sent me. For he who is least among you all—he is the greatest." (Luke 9:48, NIV)

Remember when you were young and you had faith in so much? Something happens as you age, and you let go of some of your childish beliefs. You take off the rose-colored glasses, they might say. You might do this because you have to grow up, and acting like a child indefinitely is not always the best idea. God informs us that there comes a time when you put away childish things. There is a time to become an adult. But becoming an adult should not mean letting go of your childlike faith in God.

Children are meek and humble. They trust in God unshakably. They believe He exists because adults say He does, and they feel the power of God in their hearts because they are open and receptive to Him. In today's verses, Jesus says that children are always welcome in His kingdom. Jesus wants you to have faith as you did as a child—before the world disappointed you, before you were jaded, and before you built those walls around your heart to protect yourself. Open yourself up to Jesus. Trust in Him unquestionably.

Approach Him with humility and meekness. Profess your faith to Him. Whoever welcomes the Son welcomes the Father.

Activity: How can you bring back your childlike faith? What does having a childlike faith mean to you?

December 29, 2013: Be a Committed Follower
Luke 9:57-62

Jesus replied, "No one who puts his hand to the plow and looks back is fit for service in the kingdom of God." (Luke 9:62, NIV)

A man confronts Jesus and wants to follow Jesus. Jesus tells him that he needs to let go of where he came from and move forward. The man gives Jesus two different excuses as to why he can't follow Jesus right then, so Jesus replies, "'No one who puts his hand to the plow and looks back is fit for service in the kingdom of God'" (v. 62, NIV). "To put one's hand to a plow" is an expression that signifies the undertaking of a task. In order for a plowman to finish his work, he must look onward. He cannot look back and regret what he has done. Jesus compares this to being a disciple.

If you want to undertake the task of following Jesus, you have to commit with your whole heart. You cannot continue to love the world and follow Jesus. You will continue to look back and regret the pleasures, wealth, or honors the world gives you. If you regret leaving the pleasures of the world, your heart is not dedicated to Jesus. You must renounce the ways of the world, commit wholly to Jesus, and then follow Him. If you are not willing to sacrifice everything for Christ, then you are willing to sacrifice nothing. Following Christ is all or nothing. Come to Him with your heart full of love, and give Him all you have.

Activity: End this year by assessing your life with Christ. How well did you follow Him this year? What can you do better in the coming year? Thank God for all the blessings He showered you with this year.

SECTION II

MISSIONARY SOCIETY MATERIAL
HOW TO ORGANIZE A MISSIONARY SOCIETY

Wherever any number of women desire to have a part in extending the Kingdom and will agree to give prayer, service, and offerings to missions, a Missionary Society can be organized.

Personal canvassing of the women members of the church, exhortations from the pulpit, circulation of literature, and any other means may be used to create interest and bring women together for this purpose.

FIRST: Talk with your pastor, and after securing his promise of cooperation, call a meeting of all women who would like to share in the missionary enterprise by studying, giving, and meeting together at least once a month. Be sure to invite the pastor to this meeting. Consider also inviting an experienced Baptist woman who has known missionary work through her own personal experience and, therefore, could be of assistance to you in explaining the aims of the group or in inspiring the women.

SECOND: Order a *Women's Home and Foreign Mission Society Guide and Program Book* from the R.H. Boyd Publishing Corporation. The book can be found on the R.H. Boyd Publishing Corporation Order Blank, item number 1240. It will serve as a "starter," giving you the essentials for a good foundation of organization.

The organization may be affected by the pastor, district secretary, or some well-informed women of the church. The following steps are suggested for organizing a Missionary Society:

1. Secure the cooperation of your pastor.
2. If possible, have a district secretary or conference officer present.
3. Get all necessary literature from the R.H. Boyd Publishing Corporation, 6717 Centennial Blvd., Nashville, TN 37209-1017.
4. Assemble the women by means of an announcement.

5. Have someone prepared to present the work of the Missionary Society.
6. Read and discuss membership obligations and plans for organization according to your national Baptist convention.
7. From a list of women of the church, secure names of all who will become members.
8. Select a temporary chairperson who will name a committee to nominate officers.
9. Elect and introduce officers.
10. Name all necessary committees.
11. Fix a regular time and place of meeting.
12. Send names of present and leading officers to your national convention leaders.

Why Should You Belong to a Missionary Society?

First, one should belong to a Missionary Society because Christ's last command to His disciples was, "Go ye into all the world, and preach the gospel to every creature" (Mark 16:15, KJV). He also said, "He that hath my commandments, and keepeth them, he it is that loveth me" (John 14:21, KJV). The Society is a definite place for showing love through obedience. Obedience is Christ's one test of discipleship.

Second, the Missionary Society is in keeping with God's plan to give each disciple a part in saving the world. He died for the world, and no disciple, through idleness, should fail to share the Gospel with others.

Another reason is the Society gives one an opportunity to pray in agreement with others for the spread of God's kingdom. Jesus said, "Pray ye therefore the Lord of the harvest, that he will send forth labourers" (Matt. 9:38, KJV). He also said, "If two of you shall agree on earth as touching any thing that they shall ask, it shall be done for them of my Father which is in heaven" (Matt. 18:19, KJV). Jesus loved the world for which He told His disciples to pray—so much so that He died for all humanity.

The Society not only prays for the spread of God's kingdom, but it also studies various mission fields and teaches members how God's work is progressing. God's disciples love to see His hand in the world's affairs.

In addition, the Missionary Society is adapted to the financial ability of average women. We ask them to give according to their own abilities, not those of their neighbors. If they can give only 10 cents a month, this is sufficient; if they give many times that amount, this is equally accepted and appreciated. It is a matter of rendering true stewardship in little or much. The Society shows one how small amounts saved each month become great sums for God; it makes one glad to be saving continually for Christ. The contribution, if according to the ability rule, will be accepted by Him, and He will say, "She hath done what she could" (Mark 14:8, KJV).

The Society also offers loving Christian fellowship with other women of the church. Together, the women meet to speak, pray, plan, sing, learn, and give to God and His work. When one sees the women of one's own church doing these things, she cries out, "Lord, use even me."

Finally, the Society gives a carefully planned program for reaching the poor, the erring, the indifferent, the ignorant, and the neglected of our neighborhoods.

The chief aim of all Christian work is the saving of souls. Let us actively help in the evangelistic work of our churches and strive individually to win many souls to Christ. As John Wesley once said, we have "nothing to do but to save souls."

REASONS FOR CONTRIBUTING TO THE MISSIONARY ENTERPRISE

1. Early Christians were missionaries; otherwise, Christianity would have been confined to Palestine.
2. If early missionaries had not Christianized Anglo-Saxons, we would be heathens today.
3. The price already paid to establish a worldwide Christian kingdom is so large that we cannot afford to default now.
4. If we do not Christianize other nations, they will heathenize us. We must either Christianize them or continue to fight them.
5. We would be disloyal to those of our own number, whom we have sent out, if we did not support the cause.
6. The privileges and liberties we enjoy as a race have come to us through the spreading of Christ's teachings, and further privileges and liberties will be impossible without the continued spread of Christianity.
7. The success of the past justifies our giving.
8. The missionary spirit is a vital principle of the law of life. We grow only by giving. Only missionary churches are growing.
9. Our Lord commanded it—"Go ye into all the world, and preach the gospel" (Mark 16:15, KJV). He would not have commanded us to carry on a program without requiring us to support it financially.

MISSION STATEMENT

- Empower the members of the Women's Auxiliary to carry out the Great Commission.

- Encourage greater participation in reaching out to the youth and other individuals with special needs.

- Develop home mission, foreign mission, education, and evangelism ministries to fulfill the objectives.

CONSTITUTION FOR WOMEN'S BAPTIST MISSIONARY SOCIETIES

I. Constitution for the Missionary Society

Article I

This organization shall be called the Women's Missionary Society.

Article II

Its objective shall be to foster good homes, Christian education, and home and foreign missions.

Article III

Any woman who is a regular church member in good standing may become a member of the Society by attending the meetings when possible, studying the prescribed courses, praying, and contributing each month to the causes named in the Mission Statement.

Article IV

The officers shall be a President, Vice President, Secretary, Assistant Secretary, Corresponding Secretary, Treasurer, and Chairpersons of the different committees, who shall perform the duties assigned.

Article V

The meetings shall be held weekly, at such time and place as the Society shall direct. Members pay their dues, and chairpersons make reports of work done. The week's lesson is then discussed.

Article VI

The Secretary shall send a report of accomplishments each year to the Association to which the Society belongs, the Women's Auxiliary State Convention, and the Women's Auxiliary of the National Convention.

Article VII

The Treasurer shall send all monies given for education and mission causes named each month in the Guide, keep correct and accurate accounts of all monies received and paid out, and make a quarterly report to your Society and the National Women's Auxiliary President.

II. Constitution for Society Using Circle Plan

Article I

This organization shall be the Women's Baptist Missionary Society of the ____________________ Baptist Church.

Article II

CIRCLES—The members of the local Missionary Societies may be divided into local Circles for convenience in weekly meetings. The Circles shall consist of women in the same territory if possible.

1. The officers of the Circle shall be Chairperson, elected by the Missionary Society, one Vice Chairperson, a Secretary, Treasurer, and Mission Study Leader; these are to be elected by the Circle.
2. Plan of Work—Each local Circle shall carry out the format planned by the Missionary Society.
3. Reports—Each Circle shall make a monthly written report of all work done and monies collected to the Missionary Society at its regular monthly meetings at the church. All monies on hand shall be turned over to the Missionary Society.
4. Time and Place of Meeting—Each Circle shall meet once a week; the time and place will be determined by the Circle.

ESSENTIAL COMMITTEES FOR MISSION SOCIETIES AND THEIR DUTIES

Membership—To regularly visit the women of the church, inviting them to become members. Likewise, they are to look after the absentees and welcome all who come to the meetings with a hearty handshake.

Social Committee—To arrange for special meetings, such as anniversary of organization and visit of state and national secretaries and missionaries.

Study Course Committee—To arrange for study course during the year as recommended by the Women's Convention.

Reciprocity Committee—To preserve and exchange with other societies through State Corresponding Secretaries, essays, curios, pictures, and other interesting materials.

Financial Committee—To plan special ways of increasing Society funds and special offerings for Christmas, Missions, and Education.

Lookout Committee—To gather interesting items of worldwide missions.

Decoration Committee—To have charge of arranging and beautifying the room for each weekly meeting.

Library Committee—To secure, preserve, and circulate mission books and magazines. Let this committee begin work at once even if it has a library of only one book.

Art and Museum Committee—To collect, mount, and preserve pictures of mission fields, missionaries, and curios of missionary interest.

Program Committee—To aid the President in arranging programs and seeing that they are successfully carried out.

Room Committee—To arrange the room in which the meeting is to be held and decorate with flowers when possible, which may be sent to shut-ins or hospitals after the meeting.

Visiting Committee—To collect and organize the names of all ladies in the church who do not belong to the Society and divide the list among the members. Each member is expected to visit those on her list and try to interest them in the work of the society in a spirit of love.

Literature Committee—To secure subscribers for the *UNION REVIEW*. Send subscriptions ($10.00 per year) to R.H. Boyd Publishing Corporation, 6717 Centennial Blvd., Nashville, TN 37209-1017.

Music Committee—To provide music for special occasions and, when desirable, extra music for regular meetings.

Each chairperson should make a report at every meeting. She is to use women according to their abilities. Do not appoint anyone just for the honor. All these committees are important, and the success of your Society depends greatly upon the work of these committees.

QUESTIONS AND PARLIAMENTARY RULES FOR MISSIONARY SOCIETIES

Organic and Parliamentary Law

1. **What should be the first order of business after a vote to organize a new Society?** The appointment (or election) of a committee to draw up a Constitution and Bylaws (organic laws) to be submitted at the next meeting of the society.

2. **When should the officers be elected?** Perhaps at the first meeting, but certainly in a meeting soon following. As a rule, it would be best to come to an agreement and appoint a nominating committee to suggest names for those officers for whom the Constitution provides.

3. **Should every Society have a Constitution and Bylaws?** Yes, even though the Society has been working without one. Definite statement of government and methods help to prevent confusion and misunderstanding, no matter how small the organization.

4. **What points should the Constitution cover?** (a) name; (b) object; (c) officers; (d) conditions of membership; (e) number and days of meetings; (f) quorum; (g) provisions for amendment; (h) authority in parliamentary law.

5. **What should the Bylaws cover?** All details of government and methods. Both should be as brief as possible and changed as seldom as possible.

6. **What principles underlie parliamentary procedure?** Courtesy, justice, quality, order, speed, the right of the majority to rule, and the right of the minority to be heard.

7. **Should all members of the Society be familiar with the Constitution and Bylaws and study together their authority on parliamentary laws?** Yes.

Order of Business

1. **Should a Society have a regular order of business?** Yes.

2. **What should it include?** Call to order (preferably by singing and prayer); reading and approval of minutes; reports of officers, committees, and Circles (if Circle plan is used); unfinished business; new business; announcements; and adjournment. The order of these items may be varied, and if the missionary program is to be given at the same meeting, it may precede or follow according to choice.

Quorum

1. **What is a quorum?** The number of members whose presence is necessary for the transaction of business.

2. **Why is it necessary to provide a quorum?** No business can be done unless a majority of the whole organization is present.

3. **How many constitute a quorum?** The number should be relatively small—fifteen to twenty-five for a large organization, and five to nine for a small one.

Rights and Duties of Members

Members have the right to present their propositions in the form of motions and to debate them fully.

Members shall rise when they address the Chair. It is the right of every member who notices a breach of a rule to insist upon its enforcement. She shall rise and say, "Madam Chairperson, I rise to a point of order." She will state the point of order and resume her seat. The Chair decides at once whether the point in question was "in order" or "out of order."

Members must maintain order and give courteous attention to speakers.

Elections

1. **How may members be nominated for office?** (a) By a nominating committee; (b) by nominations from the floor; (c) or by "informal ballot" (slips of paper upon which each member writes her choice).

2. **What, on the whole, has proved the most satisfactory method of nominating officers in a Women's Missionary**

Society? Nominations by a nominating committee of one name for each office.

3. **As a rule, how is the nominating committee selected?** By nominating from the floor and election by voice ("aye" and "no").

4. **Should the nominating committee secure the consent of its nominees before reporting?** Yes.

5. **After the nominating committee has presented the names of its nominees, should the opportunity be given for nominations from the floor?** Yes.

6. **How may too many nominations be prevented?** By the motion to "close nominations."

7. **When should a nominee decline if she cannot serve?** As soon as she is nominated.

8. **If there is more than one nominee for each office, how should the election be held?** By ballot.

9. **If there is but one nominee for each office, how may she be elected?** By voice, but the society should have specified in the Constitution and Bylaws that this method can be used, or by (unanimous) vote in small societies.

10. **Does accepting the committees' report elect the officers?** No, the vote to "accept" the report simply accepts the names presented as nominees of the Society, who then elects by the method previously decided upon.

11. **Is it best to fill offices one by one?** As a rule, but not necessarily.

12. **Should the method of nominating and electing officers be specified in the Bylaws?** Yes.

13. **If the Constitution and/or Bylaws provide for a nominating committee to nominate officers, should the method of choosing the committee also be specified?** Yes.

Motion

All business shall be brought before an assembly by a motion. When a member makes a motion, it should not be debated or acted upon unless it has been seconded. She should say, "Madam President, I move that..." She should not say, "I make a motion that..." or "I move that..."

When a motion is seconded, the President shall distinctly state the motion and shall put the question thus: "All who are in favor say 'aye.'" Then the president shall say, "All who are opposed say 'no.'" The President shall announce that the motion is carried or lost.

Any motion can be amended by adding to, inserting, or striking out a part; but the amendment cannot be acted on unless seconded.

An amendment shall **always** be voted on before the original question. If lost, then the original motion is considered; but if the amendment is carried, the President shall say, "All who are in favor of the motion as amended say, 'Aye,'" etc.

An amendment can be offered to an amendment, but no further amendment is in order. When an amendment to an amendment is offered, it must be acted on first; then, the amendment must be acted on, and finally the original motion.

Amendments

1. **What is an amendment?** A change in the meaning of the motion.

2. **May a change that is just a change in word but not in meaning be made without a motion to amend?** Yes. **By whom?** The Chair.

3. **How many amendments may there be to a motion at one time?** Two. A primary amendment and then a motion to amend the (primary) amendment, which is called the secondary amendment.

4. **How many times must the society vote when two amendments are pending?** Three. First, the vote on the secondary amendment; second, the vote on the primary amendment as amended if the secondary amendment has carried or as it was first

stated if the secondary amendment was not carried; third, the vote on the main question as amended or as it was at first if the primary amendment is lost.

5. **May an amendment be accepted without vote? If so, by whom?** Yes, by the one making the motion; but if anyone objects, the amendment must be put to a vote.

6. **What are the three methods of amendments?** (a) Inserting or adding new words; (b) striking out words; (c) striking out words and inserting or adding new words in their place.

7. **When an amendment consists of a whole new motion or phrase, what is it called?** A substitute.

Reconsider, Rescind

1. **How may a question that has been voted upon be reopened?** By a motion to reconsider.

2. **Who only may make this motion?** One of the members who voted with the majority when the motion was carried or lost.

3. **Does debate upon the motion to reconsider open debate on the original question?** Yes.

4. **What is the effect if the motion to reconsider is carried?** It cancels the vote that had been taken and gives opportunity for further discussion and another vote. If lost, the original decision stands.

5. **When may the motion to reconsider be made?** At the same meeting or the following.

6. **When voted for the second time, is it finally settled?** Yes.

7. **Can nominations and elections be reconsidered?** No.

8. **Is the motion to rescind the same as the motion to reconsider?** No. Reconsideration reopens the question for action and a second vote; rescinding cancels the vote, and no further action on that question is taken.

9. **Should notice of intention to rescind be given?** Yes, to every member.

Special Committees

1. A Committee usually consists of three or five members and is appointed by the President, elected by nomination and vote, or chosen by ballot.

2. The first person named by the President is considered the convener of the committee, and the committee by a majority of its members may elect a chairperson.

3. When the committee is expected to report at the same meeting, it shall at once retire and agree upon a report, which should be written out. Upon its return, the chairperson of the committee reads the report and hands it to the presiding officer, at which time a committee member or some other member may move to adopt the report or to amend it. Such motions, if carried, become the resolution of the assembly just as if the committee had nothing to do with them.

A report is received when read. The reception of a report does not mean its adoption. The report can be amended and modified and is subject to all proper motions.

4. When a committee to nominate officers is ready to report, the President may conduct the election or she may request another to take the chair. A good parliamentarian who can do the work well and quickly should be used.

5. In all times of perplexity, the President should remember the advice of an authority on parliamentary law who said, "The great purpose of all rules and forms is to subserve the will of the assembly, rather than to restrain it; to facilitate, and not to obstruct, the expression of their delicate sense" (Luther Cushing, *Manual of Parliamentary Practice).*

SUGGESTED ORDER OF SERVICE FOR THE MISSIONARY MEETING

1. **Devotional**—Always begin the meeting with a message from God's Word, prayer, and singing.

2. **Reading of secretary's minutes**—The President will then ask if there are any corrections to be made. If there are, she will receive them. If not, she will state that the minutes are approved.

3. **The treasurer's report**—She will state how much money has been received since her last report and for what purpose, as well as how much she has on hand. The President will then call for

the acceptance of this report. Someone will move its acceptance, someone else will second it, and the society will vote.

4. **Business**—Business should be presented through committee reports and recommendations to save time that would otherwise be consumed by discussion of details in the meeting. Do not let the business take program time.

5. **The program**—Let this be prepared carefully. Put your best effort into it. Every year, a set of most interesting programs is suggested in your *Women's Home and Foreign Mission Guide* by editorial experts. It is recommended to all Program Committees that they use these materials as a background for their regular lessons. Any Circle, however, which chooses to use other material in addition to that suggested in the *Guide* is at liberty to do so. Remember, your society is not for entertainment or amusement, but for information, for work, and for inspiration to do God's work better. Work as hard for the success of the missionary meeting as you do for your literary society or any social club, for the Missionary Society is more important than all these other things. The evangelization of countless souls depends on its success.

6. **Form of closing**—Close with several short prayers, the petition of the Women's Missionary Pledge, which every member should know by heart, and the missionary hymn.

7. **Learn to think on your feet and to speak extemporaneously.** Have no fear. Be fully aware of your subject; try to be natural, and you will be guided by the Holy Spirit. Remember that you are to please Christ with your words and your message, and you will forget your audience in striving to please Him.

8. **Remember that the best president or chairperson of a committee is the one who gets the most out of others.** There may be great ability in your society, which you can find only by drawing it out. Try out new people from time to time. Do not let a few do all the work.

9. **Have plenty of the right kind of music.** There are many beautiful missionary hymns from which to draw. Do not choose all jazz

or popular swing type jubilees. Have some reverent and dignified church hymns in your repertoire.

10. **Allow plenty of time in your meetings for prayer.** Interrupt the program occasionally to pray for the subject of your study. Do not be afraid to ask the women to offer prayer, but unless they are accustomed to doing so in public, speak to them before the meeting. Remember, Jesus said, "Without me ye can do nothing" (John 15:5, KJV). Organize "prayer bands" of women who will engage in private daily prayer concerning special objects of need or special fields of missionary endeavor.

WHY HAVE MISSIONARY SOCIETIES?

1. Because Jesus Christ commanded that missionary work be done throughout the world, and upon His resurrection said to the women, "Go tell" (Matt. 28:10, KJV). Mary started telling the Good News at the opened tomb, and women must still carry the Gospel message in obedience to Jesus' command.
2. Because organizations get work done quicker than individuals do, and they cover larger territories.
3. Because organizations represent opportunities to discover leadership and talent and to develop both.
4. Because the world needs evangelism and Christian civilization. This cannot be accomplished by individuals alone but through the intelligent, consecrated cooperation of Christian believers.
5. Because it offers many opportunities for enlightenment, the enlisting of sympathy, and the attainment of the objectives of the Christian church.
6. Because the Missionary Society offers a great opportunity for the ironing out of interracial difficulties and misunderstandings. The women in the churches of all races have more courage to meet the situation on the interracial front today than almost any other group in religious life.
7. Because through the work and study of a Missionary Society, men, women, and children come to know Jesus as their Savior, through whom knowledge must come about the kingdom of God.

WHAT YOUR SOCIETY OR CIRCLE SHOULD BE DOING RIGHT NOW

1. It should enlist every member in the church who believes that the whole world needs the whole Gospel and that God wants them to have an active part in such a program.

2. It should teach challenging missionary lessons from the Bible at least once a month.

3. It should study the lives of missionary heroines and heroes and draw lessons therefrom.

4. It should present the story of missions in addresses and pageants at least once a quarter.

5. It should know the names of missionaries in the field, where they are working, what they are doing, and what their needs are.

6. It should pray for missionaries by name and contribute personally to the work of at least one station.

7. It should know and give intelligently and regularly. It should follow up its gifts—not blindly or spasmodically.

8. It should subscribe to at least one missionary magazine and get reports from the Mission Board.

9. It should study and analyze these reports, seeking additional information from the Board if necessary.

10. It should vote on and distribute the money for definite purposes and get receipts for same.

11. It should occasionally invite returned missionaries and get firsthand information.

12. If the Society is not pleased with the reports heard or read, it should take the matter up with the Board through which it makes its contributions.

13. Its members should not talk to other members about what they do not like; rather, they should talk to the Secretary of their Board of Missions and then act.

14. Its officers should make written reports to the church at least once a year.

15. It is the duty of members to find young people who might make fine leaders and contribute to their education in a Christian school that offers courses for Christian social service.

16. Its members should talk less about "nothing" and do more about the cause.

17. It should not stand still. "Forward with God" should be the catch phrase.

18. It should have a Missionaries' bookshelf and reading table at a convenient place in the church and should keep adding new material, books, and magazines.

INSTALLATION OF OFFICERS

In secret societies and in many other organizations outside the church, special prominence is given to the installation of officers. Why? The new officers are unable to perform their duties unless informed what these duties are. Also, public recognition is due them and often proves a source of real encouragement as they begin to fill positions of leadership. In addition, it is a good opportunity to make officers aware of their stewardship to God and the need to consecrate themselves for His service and His glory.

It is of more importance for the officers of the Women's Missionary Societies to understand their duties than it is for those of secular organizations to know what they are to do. Many think it is not important, but practice has shown the installation service to be of great benefit in our local churches. It is considered an important calling to be selected as an officer in so far-reaching an endeavor as the work of the Women's Missionary Program in our Baptist churches. In order that each officer be prepared to meet her obligations, it is essential that she be fully instructed as to what her duties are.

It is suggested that, after new officers have been elected, they be called together to map out plans and devise ways and means for the new year's effort. In this way, the President and her assistants will be in a position to present some definite policy of work, some goal in view at the very first meeting of their new year.

After this has been done during the first meeting, it is good to include, along with the installation of officers, instructions for new officers in regard to assuming their duties intelligently. A service of commission and prayer is recommended.

Deciding who shall conduct this service is not as important as ensuring that it is conducted in the manner and spirit intended. In some instances, the pastor might be the best person to do it. However, the district superintendent, a state mission board officer, the retiring president, or some member of the auxiliary might be chosen as the most desirable person to act as leader on this occasion. In any case, the one selected should realize his or her responsibility and enter into the sacredness of this service in the spirit of prayer and consecration. If conducted in a half-hearted manner, it might as well be omitted from the missionary program.

PERSONAL SERVICE OR COMMUNITY MISSIONS

"Behold, I say unto you, Lift up your eyes, and look on the fields; for they are white already to harvest" (John 4:35, KJV).

When Stradivarius, a famous violin maker, was asked how long it took to form a violin, he replied, "A thousand years!" He also said that violins made from trees shielded from storms could never be made into a masterpiece. Because of the intangible adaptability of its nature, personal service cannot be measured by rules. As a tree must be subjected to time and the elements before being used to make a violin, so our hearts must be tempered by love and strengthened by faith. Service, without the giving of oneself, becomes an empty gift; and personal service, without presenting the Savior, loses all its meaning.

Organized personal service does not merely mean standardized work. If it were so, our task would be easier; but it would lose much of its joy and charm. As each violin has a different tone, so each of us has a different sphere of service. The object, however, is the same—harmony in the world of music for the violin; harmony with God's plan for us.

First, as always, must come soul-winning. To bring to Christ those who are now lost and who need Him so desperately is joy incomparable. For each of our talents, there is a place of service waiting, and God, in His infinite wisdom, will surely point out the way. It has been decided that societies will no longer report the number of conversions but will merely confirm that they are engaged in definite efforts for soul-winning. Each society is urged to make soul-winning its chief objective.

Second, the community missions program furnishes a delightful manner in which individuals in a Missionary Society may extend some small, useful gift of service to another individual in a personal way. Every community offers some field for this type of service, and alert Missionary Society members will discern the needs of others and will respond to them accordingly. Special work for prisoners, invalids, and shut-ins may be classified as personal service.

Are there people in need in your community? Perhaps there are children who are ashamed to attend Sunday school or Starlight Band because they lack proper clothing or their clothes are in need of repair. Sickness of the mother in that family, or other conditions, may make this service the duty of an outsider. Perhaps there is a family that would greatly benefit from a special gift, a pretty quilt, or a table linen. Perhaps there are ladies who could benefit from your sewing ability. Is your women's organization meeting such needs? The help given should not be regarded as "charity." Rather, it is an expression of the true missionary, who loves to serve and meet human needs as Jesus did.

Christmas Needs

To the missionaries themselves, you may send dainty personal gifts to serve as reminders of your interest in them and their work. Any missionary would be delighted to receive something pretty to wear, of the best quality and just the right size, or something attractive for her home. Even more valuable than the gift would be the joy of knowing that someone cares enough to remember her.

COMMUNITY MISSIONS

The late Dr. Fannie C. Thompson made the following statements concerning the fourfold purpose of **COMMUNITY MISSIONS:**

1. To enlist all women and young people of the church in definite missionary activity within the community, with soul-winning and other spiritual results as the desired ends.

2. To promote evangelism in cooperation with the Women's Missionary Convention plans, engaging in such evangelistic activities as Cottage Prayer Meetings, Goodwill Centers, and services in institutions.

3. To manifest Christian fellowship through making contact with indifferent Christians, ministering to the sick, and helping men and women in the armed forces in the community.

4. To emphasize those moral standards which pertain to community life: high standards of dress; speech and conduct; Christian observance of Sunday; total abstinence at home and in the community; establishment of family altars; measures of public health and child welfare; improvement of industrial conditions and observance of the law; and emphasis of racial justice through cooperative agencies.

THE WHY AND HOW OF A MISSION STUDY CLASS

1. Aims and Objectives of a Mission Study Course

A. To KNOW more about the people of the world and their spiritual needs.

B. To CARE that people everywhere come to know Christ.

C. To PRAY for our missionaries, the native workers, and the fields.

D. To GIVE through the church missionary program, the Women's Auxiliary offering, gleaners, etc.

E. To GO, if the Lord calls, to special fields of work in your community, homeland, or the uttermost part of the country under discussion.

2. What the Mission Study Chairperson Should Know

A. She should know what the mission class is. (a) It is not a book review. (b) It is not a lecture. (c) It is a group of two or more, including a leader, that meets for discussion which grows out of a previous reading of the book used as a basis of study. Therefore, the Mission Study chairperson should urge all members to buy and read each book studied.

B. She should know the books in the course of study, as outlined for the year by the Women's Auxiliary.

C. She should inform herself of new mission study books being published.

3. When to Have Mission Study Class

A. In a special "extra" meeting—not just sandwiched in the regular meeting between program and business. Longer books may require two or more meetings to complete discussion.

B. In church schools of missions when the entire church is engaged in mission institute or study courses.

C. In cooperation with other churches in the community or the city.

It would be fine to have at least two classes each year in each Circle, in addition to a wide reading of missionary books on the part of members of the group.

4. How to Conduct a Mission Study Class

A. Choose a book suitable for the ages in the group and not too long for the time allowed.

B. Pray; read the book; reread book and assembled materials; outline plans; prepare each lesson in detail; plan the assignments.

C. Advertise class early in the newspaper, church bulletins, posters, vestibule, Sunday school classrooms, announcements from the pulpit, personal invitations or letters, and phone calls.

D. Class period—begin and close on time. Have occasional supper meetings, with a period before and after supper. Use members. Give illustrations. Stimulate discussions.

E. Reach the minds and hearts of members. Relate teaching to their lives. Bring the work of your national convention close to the class. Stimulate the giving and living of members.

SECTION III

MAKING MISSIONS INTERESTING

A. The Use of Missionary Letters

Societies should band together and pass around a good missionary letter so the words of the missionary go as far as possible. The missionary committees of the same denomination in a city or in neighboring small towns should cooperate to this end. Duplicating missionary letters is not recommended because it takes the personality out of them. It is better to pass the originals around. Be sure to pass on the foreign envelope with the stamp and postmark. As these letters go to the various societies, how delightful it would be for each society to write to the missionary (some member should be instructed to oversee this task).

B. A Story Three Yards Long

For a Japanese meeting, have a paper with the above title written on it. Use a sheet of paper about five or six inches wide and three yards long. (Of course, it may be any number of feet or yards long, according to the length desired.) When the story is written, begin at the end and roll it up. In reading, do not unroll it any faster than you read.

Japanese letter paper often comes in rolls, and letters are written by the foot or yard.

C. A Missionary Quiz

The scope of the missionary quiz must be announced several weeks beforehand so members can study. It is best conducted by the pastor, who will manage it in the same way as the old-fashioned spelling bee. Instead of requiring participants to spell English words, the pastor will ask them questions about missionary history and other missionary facts. If teams are chosen three or four weeks in advance, the leaders may be trusted to see that the members of their respective teams are well-posted before the evening arrives. Confine the questions to one country or one missionary board. It might be good to give a quality missionary book to the victor, but this should be a surprise.

D. An Animated Missionary Library

Each woman is to represent a missionary book. She will study the contents of the book, and at the social she will answer all questions with reference to it. The books will be given numbers, and the women will pick numbers without knowing to which books the numbers correspond. Then, the conversation will begin between the woman with the number and the woman who studied the book and will continue until the woman has discovered the book about which the other is talking. Then, she may draw another number.

E. A Missionary Worker's Creed

1. I believe in God the Father Almighty, Maker of heaven and earth;
2. And in Jesus Christ, His only Son, our Lord, who was born of the Virgin Mary and died in our stead as an atoning sacrifice for sin.
3. I believe that He rose from the dead in human body; and ascended to heaven therein.
4. I believe that He will return visibly in judgment to raise the dead and reign forever in the glorified body, as the everlasting incarnation of God.
5. I believe in the Holy Spirit, who exists eternally with the Father and the Son in the unity of the Godhead and regenerates and sanctifies the penitent through faith in Christ.
6. I believe that the Holy Bible is the Word of God, the supreme authority in religion; and in the light of all the facts concerning it, without errors of any kind, except small literary ones in the translations.
7. I believe that man was created by special divine act but sinned when tempted of the devil and incurred spiritual and physical death.
8. I believe that those who accept the Lord Jesus Christ as their Redeemer are saved while those who reject Him will suffer the eternal consequence of sin in hell.
9. I believe that the Church universal is the company of all who are redeemed by the blood of Christ and are formed by the Holy Spirit into one spiritual body, of which Christ alone is the Head.

10. I believe that it is the mission of the Church to share Christ's death and resurrection through personal faith in Him, as signified by baptism; to glorify Him by good works; to give His gospel to all people; to wait for His appearing; and to partake of the Lord's Supper until He comes.

F. Suggestions for Service

For every member of the Missionary Society who wishes to do something to help the Master, there are one hundred jobs to be done. Never let anyone hear you say, "Well, I just can't do anything at all because I do not have any talent to use."

"Let none hear you idly saying,
'There is nothing I can do,'
While the souls of men are dying
And the Master calls for you.
Take the task He gives you gladly,
Let His work your pleasure be;
Answer quickly when He calleth,
'Here am I, send me, send me!'"

— Daniel March

Visit the sick. If you cannot do this, call the pastor on the telephone and tell him of cases of sickness about which you may have heard. Make sick members feel that they are not forgotten.

Remember shut-ins. Occasionally, write them letters telling them of some good points in the pastor's sermons or sharing church news. Arrange a small group to visit the home of a shut-in and hold a brief service there.

Use your automobile. There are elderly people in most churches who rarely attend church because they lack transportation. You can help them by both taking them to church and taking them home after the service. You can also use your automobile to run errands for shut-in members. These are simple services that should be done!

Hold an Old-Folks' Day at your church. One afternoon, entertain all the elderly people who come. Give out special invitations beforehand. Call to confirm who will come. On the day of the event, pick up guests and take them to the church. Have suitable entertainment—tea, refreshments, singing, brief and happy talks, and a general good time for the elderly folks.

Serve in an every-member canvass. Most churches need workers for this. Perhaps it can be a survey of the district arranged by the pastor. Offer your services as a society or individually.

Provide a literature table on the church porch. To do this, first get the consent of the pastor and church officers. Collect suitable magazines and place them on the table weekly. Church members will gladly give their magazines for this purpose. Anyone may take home a magazine but must return it the next week. For this to be a successful activity, it must be taken seriously. A neglected magazine table falls into disrepute. It must be kept in good shape.

Distribute tracts or invitations to attend church service. These may be given out from house to house or in hotels.

Make posters advertising church services. Place them in shop windows, railroad stations, barbershops, etc.

Teach classes in the Sunday church school. Form a teachers' training class in which participants will learn how to teach. Study the Sunday school lesson weekly to be ready to substitute for any absent teacher.

Go out and bring in boys and girls to form new classes in the Sunday church school. If there are few children in your church, find out why and bring them in.

Read denominational literature. Try to get subscriptions to the ***Union Review*** and the ***Study Course and Manual.***

Be a Big Brother or Sister. Assist some of the youth who need help of any kind.

Form an orchestra to serve in the church's evening service.

Keep the church grounds in order.

Attend the church Sunday evening service as a Missionary Society.

Provide flowers for the church services Sunday morning.

Clean up. Paint the inside of the church and keep the kitchen clean.

Supply needed equipment. This might include chairs, carpet, curtains, hymnals, etc. Take down, clean, and replace curtains in the rooms of the church.

Keep the windows clean.

Serve at church banquets, picnics, etc.

During the summer months, plan picnics for the elderly and lonely.

SECTION IV

MATERIAL FOR MOTHERS' UNION

(An organization for mothers of young and adolescent children)

Purpose

The object of the Mothers' Union is to bring mothers together in every church and community to discuss the problems and methods of rearing children and to help make the home, community, and church life better. Its underlying purpose is to make the home life Christian, so each child is given an opportunity from the days of his or her youth to know Jesus as Lord and Savior. While the Union is primarily for mothers of the young, any woman who is interested in the welfare of the youth and the home may become a member by fulfilling the conditions of membership as outlined in Article III of the Mothers' Union Constitution.

ORDER OF BUSINESS FOR MEETING

Devotional Exercises (including Scripture reading, one or two hymns or spirituals, and prayer), roll call, payment of love offering and dues, and reading of minutes by Recording Secretary.

Treasurer's Report

Report of Standing Committees

Report of Special Committees

Unfinished Business

(Learn to not waste one minute of your meeting time on a worthless matter. Rule out all personal discussions.)

PROGRAM TIME

(Leaders for the week will take charge here.)

Lessons from the *Guide*

Reading and Explanation of Scripture

Suggestions from the Lesson

Practical Outcomes of Lesson

Adjournment

Closing Prayer

CONSTITUTION FOR MOTHERS' UNION

Article I

This organization shall be known as the Mothers' Union of ______________________________ Church.

Article II

Its object shall be to organize a Mothers' Union in every church and community—to help make the home, community, and church life better.

Article III

Any woman who is a mother or any woman interested in the welfare of children may become a member by attending the meetings when possible, studying the prescribed course, praying and contributing to the causes named in the *Guide,* and distributing religious and health tracts to families.

Article IV

The officers shall be President, Vice President, Recording Secretary, Assistant Recording Secretary, Corresponding Secretary, Treasurer, and Chairperson of different committees who shall perform the duties assigned to such officers.

Article V

The meetings shall be held weekly at such time and place as the Union shall direct; members pay their dues, make reports of work done by Chairperson, and discuss the week's lesson.

Article VI

The Secretary shall send a report of accomplishments each year to the appropriate organization within the state convention and national convention.

1. Unions—Once a month, all Mothers' Unions will meet together at the church to make written reports and plan further for the work. All on hand shall be turned over to the Mothers' Union.

2. Time and place of meeting—Each Union shall meet once a week; the time and place should be determined by the Union.

Article VII—Committee

1. **Enlistment**—It shall be the duty of this committee to visit every home and enlist every mother in some active work for the church and to enlist the mothers in missionary education and benevolent work. Look up absent mothers and try to secure a full attendance at each meeting of the Mothers' Union and the monthly meetings.

2. **Social**—Welcome mothers and visit newcomers to your neighborhood. Plan socials to entertain the mothers and have helpful programs about making our homes Christian, intellectual, cheerful, happy, and beautiful. Sponsor health programs and better home programs several times a year.

3. **Benevolent**—Visit and aid sick and needy mothers. Visit hospitals, deliver flowers, and give helpful articles whenever needed.

4. **Missionary and Educational**—Encourage Bible study and the right kind of literature for the family. Encourage the mothers to send their children to Sunday church school, Starlight Band, Girls' Auxiliary, Shepherd Boys' League, and public schools and Christian institutions. Secure subscriptions for the denominational paper and distribute among Mothers' Unions along with tracts and good magazines. Also deliver them to the families of women represented in the Union.

5. **Industrial**—Plan a sewing circle to help mothers sew and mend articles for their families. Have meetings to encourage the better rearing of children, keeping of homes, and beautifying of both front and back yards.

MOTHERS' UNION EMBLEMS

1. The color for the Mothers' Union is purple.

2. The Mothers' Union button has the letters "M.U. of (*the initials of the convention*)" around the button and the words "We Are Helpers" in the center of the button. The lettering is white.

SPECIAL COMMITTEES AND DUTIES FOR MOTHERS' UNIONS

Membership—To visit each mother in your community (making the canvass by streets and blocks) and invite each to become a member of the Mothers' Union.

Visiting Committee—The names of all mothers in each community, not merely members of a Mothers' Union, should be divided. Each member is expected to visit those on her list and try to interest them in Mothers' Union work.

Literature Committee—To supply mothers with *Guides* and Mothers' Union buttons as well as health and Christian tracts.

Program Committee—To arrange suitable programs for Mothers' meetings in which the family altar, home life, and the rearing of children will be emphasized.

Financial Committee—To arrange programs and ways and means to raise funds to help supply needs of Mothers' Unions.

TEN QUALITIES FOR MOTHERS

The ideal mother is (1) spiritual; (2) independent; (3) intelligent; (4) conscientious; (5) tolerant; (6) assertive; (7) social; (8) consecrated; (9) self-sacrificing; (10) heroic.

Helping Your Child Know the Bible

Many parents ask, "What should we teach our children about the Bible? When should we begin?" The answer to these questions in regard to "what" and "when" are found in the answer to another one: "Why should we teach our children the Bible?" We know that the Bible is the greatest book in the world, and anyone unfamiliar with it is not truly educated. But the reason is deeper than that. The Bible tells the greatest story in the world—humanity's search for God and God's love for humanity. The Bible is the Word of God, a message from God to humanity. It is a source of help in times of need and of inspiration at all times. Anything we do to introduce children to the Bible must lead to their appreciation of it in all its greatness. However, this is not as easy as it might seem.

The Bible in the Home

Children may enjoy the stories in the Bible but still develop a feeling that it is not as important a book as the one they see their mother reading with great interest or their father studying eagerly as he seeks to improve himself in his particular field of work.

The best way for children to be introduced to the Bible is by seeing it in the home as a book highly valued by their parents, studied with interest, and read aloud with satisfaction.

An Adventure Together

Families have many interesting experiences together. None of them will be more thrilling than studying the Bible, seeking to find God's way, and walking in it.

The Bible in People

The Bible is a living book, but it truly lives today only when it lives in people who love God and seek to do His will. Children will read it with greater interest if they have first seen it in the lives of the people they know.

Ways of Using the Bible

After children are familiar with the appearance of the Bible as both a book and a library of books, their introduction to its contents may be through books of Bible stories.

A book of Bible stories to read to children should have a place in any family in which the fine art of reading aloud is cultivated. The knowledge that children gain through the study of the Bible is an important part of their total education.

Lesson folders and study booklets, which children bring home from their church schools, contain Bible stories and verses that have been selected for children their age. They make it possible for parents to guide the children's home Bible study and can be used in family worship. Additionally, books that explain the customs and living conditions of Bible times help make biblical people and places real. By the time children are eight years old, they enjoy looking things up in reference books that are not too difficult.

Reading the Bible

Nothing can take the place of reading the Bible, aloud or privately, and every family should have a good copy with print large enough for children to read. A modern translation will add interest to the reading. Consider the *Revised Standard Version of the Bible*; *An American New Translation* by Goodspeed and Smith; *The Bible,* a new translation by James Moffatt; or, for clarity, *The Living Bible*.

The Sunday school may provide each child with a Bible when the child enters the junior department or fourth grade. If not, parents will wish to do so and should obtain the version used in the child's class.

The Difference Between a Mothers' Board and a Mothers' Union

It is wise to keep in mind the difference between a Mothers' Board and a Mothers' Union. The Mothers' Board, usually called the Mothers' Board of the Church, is composed of elderly mothers or motherly women who are members of the church and to whom the younger generation looks for guidance, inspiration, comfort, and counsel.

The Mothers' Union differs from the Mothers' Board as it is composed chiefly of younger mothers, usually with small or adolescent children. The Mothers' Union gathers together for the purpose of studying ways and methods of raising and nurturing their children in a manner well-pleasing to God. One of the purposes of this page is to show the differences between these two working groups of women. Any average- or large-size church may have both of these groups working and will find their programs do not overlap. Also, many Mothers' Unions have been organized by Christian women in the neighborhood of the church; many of the women who make up these Unions are not members of this or that church but merely young mothers who need the inspiration and fellowship of other mothers who face similar problems with their children. It is to be remembered, however, that the Mothers' Board is always organized through the church, for the service of the church, and chiefly inside the church.

When Families Pray

The influence of a family can reach around the world when it is united in prayer and worship in the home.

There is power in prayer. A family is never stronger than when united in prayer during family worship. During family worship, objects of prayer should be chosen carefully to ensure that no needy and worthy causes are overlooked.

The Church needs our prayers. The verdict of every praying Christian is that prayer changes things, and prayer can change a church. Families can use the power of prayer to help churches grow in grace and win more souls for Christ.

We should pray for others. When we channel our prayers in the direction of others, we are not merely inducing God to grant favors to those for whom we pray. We are also showing we are interested in them and are submitting that interest to God for His divine approval and purification.

At the same time, we are making ourselves receptive to His power. The floodgates of His divine grace will open wide and pour that grace into our minds and hearts. He will energize the lives of those we pray for, making it easier for them to know and feel the will of God.

We should pray for our families. It is an opportunity to mention the names and needs of our family members, requesting God's sovereign intervention on their behalf.

If we pray for the members of our family in their presence, they will know that we care. Those who care for each other become linked together in love.

SECTION V

FOR BIBLE BAND AND UNION

STATEMENT OF PURPOSE

The object of the Bible Band is to organize and encourage systematic Bible study in homes, organizations, and churches; to establish family altars in the homes; and to see that every family is provided with a Bible, one for each member of the family if possible.

Dr. M. A. B. Fuller (1869-1972) was a great pioneer, leader, motivator, and Christian worker. In the half-century that she worked with the Women's Missionary Auxiliary of the National Baptist Convention of America, she pointed the mission workers to greater faithfulness and higher thinking and living in many vital, vibrant ways. In 1928, in Shreveport, La., Dr. Fuller organized the Junior Women's Auxiliary, which rapidly developed into a progressive national organization. She could do many things well, and she did her best in all of them. Her service was endless.

Though her mortal life has passed, her immortal influence will never die. She will always be remembered for her contribution and dedicated service rendered to thousands across the country.

CONSTITUTION FOR LOCAL BIBLE BANDS

Article I

This organization shall be known as the Bible Band of the ______________________________ Church.

Article II

Its object shall be to organize and encourage systematic Bible study in the homes, organizations, and churches; to establish family altars in the homes; and to see that every family is provided with a Bible, one for each member of the family if possible.

Article III

Any woman who is a regular church member in good standing may become a member of the Band by attending meetings whenever possible, reading the Bible daily, and studying the prescribed course. Men may become honorary members.

Article IV

The officers shall be a President, Vice President, Recording Secretary, Assistant Recording Secretary, Treasurer, and also Chairpersons of different committees who shall perform the duties assigned to them.

Article V

The meetings shall be held weekly at such time and place as the Band shall direct. Members pay their dues and make reports of work done by the Chairpersons.

Article VI

The Corresponding Secretary shall send a report of all accomplishments each year to the appropriate organization within their state convention and national convention.

Article VII

The Treasurer shall send monies given for Education and Mission causes named each month in the *Guide*, keep a correct and accurate account of all monies received and paid out, and make a quarterly report to the following: the Bible Band, the Women's State Convention, and the Women's Auxiliary of the National Convention. A report shall also be sent to the Corresponding Secretaries of these organizations.

CONSTITUTION FOR BIBLE BAND USING CIRCLE PLAN

Article I

This organization shall be known as the Women's Bible Band of the ____________________ Church.

Article II

Its object shall be to organize and encourage systematic Bible study in the homes, organizations, and churches; to establish family altars in the homes; and to see that every family is provided with a Bible, one for each member of the family if possible.

Article III

Any woman who is a regular church member in good standing may become a member of the Circle by attending the meetings whenever possible, reading the Bible daily, and studying the prescribed course. Men may become honorary members, and any person who does not belong to the Baptist church may also become an honorary member.

Article IV

The officers shall be President, Vice President, Secretary, Assistant Secretary, Corresponding Secretary, and Treasurer, who shall perform the duties assigned to such officers.

Article V

Circle—The members of the Local Band may be divided into local Circles for convenience in weekly meetings. The Circle shall consist of members in the same community if possible.

1. **Officers**—The Officers elected by the Bible Band Circle shall be President, Vice President, Secretary, Treasurer, and Bible Study Leader.

2. **Plan of Work**—Each local Bible Band Circle shall carry out the work as planned by the Bible Band.

3. **Reports**—Each Bible Band Circle shall make a monthly written report of all work done and monies collected for the Bible Band at its regular monthly meetings at the church. All collected monies on hand shall be turned over to the Bible Band Organization Treasurer.

4. **Time and Place of Meeting**—Each Bible Band Circle shall meet once a week; the time and place will be determined by the Bible Band.

ESSENTIAL COMMITTEES FOR BIBLE BANDS

Membership—Visit the homes in your neighborhood; try to influence every person to read the Bible daily and become a member of the Bible Band.

Visiting Committee—Get the names of the families in the neighborhood, divide them, and give a certain number of names to each member. Each member is expected to visit those on her list, try to enlist them to join the Band and read the Bible, and pray with them.

Literature Committee—Supply members with Bibles, guides, other Christian books and papers, Bible Band Buttons, and tracts.

HISTORY OF BIBLE BAND

There is no power strong enough to reform human lives but the great and unparalleled power of the Gospel of the Son of God. And there is no book that tells about this Gospel but the Bible. Therefore, the great object in all our work has been to get this book into the hands and hearts of all. This great thought led up to the present Band. The very first Bible Band grew out of the missionary work of Miss Joanna P. Moore. In 1888, Miss Moore wrote that 90 Bands with 1,638 members had reported being organized, and in 1889, many more were organized. Bible Bands were really the forerunners of the present Women's Missionary Societies. Whenever Miss Moore organized Bible Bands, she also taught the women the great missionary teachings of the Bible because the two go hand in hand.

The object of the organization is to study and commit to memory the Word of God for personal edification and comfort; to teach it to others; and, if possible, to supply Bibles to every man, woman, and child who can read. No organization would have been required if people had already been gathering to study the Bible and to encourage each other. It is the duty of each member of the Bible Band to read or hear read a chapter, or a part of a chapter, each day and commit to memory new verses each week. Every Bible Band member should carry a Bible with her whenever she goes to church or to any meeting. It is also a good plan to keep a small Testament in your pocket while at work so that you may study God's Word in leisure moments.

BIBLE BAND EMBLEM

1. Bible Band color is black.
2. The textbook of the Bible Band is the Bible itself.
3. The Bible Band button is a yellow enameled button with the letters "B.B. of (*the initials of the convention*)" around the button and the words "Thy Will Be Done" in the center of the button on a Bible. The lettering is black.

BIBLE BAND PRAYER

"Oh God, help me to remember that Thou art talking to me when I read the Bible, and may I believe every word Thou sayest. May the Holy Spirit shine in my heart and make the meaning plain; make me willing to obey all Thy commands for Jesus' sake—Amen."

RULES FOR READING THE BIBLE
(By Miss Joanna P. Moore, Founder of Bible Band)

1. If I am a SAVED sinner, I should stop at every promise for a Christian and ask if I believe it and rest my soul upon it; at every command, I should ask if I obey it cheerfully (Luke 6:46; John 14:15; 15:14).
2. If I am an UNSAVED sinner, I should stop at every invitation of mercy and ask my own heart why I do not accept it. Likewise, I should remember that God will accept no service nor work of my hands till I receive the pardon of my sins that Jesus bought with His own blood. I need only to accept and believe His promise, and then, I am a SAVED sinner (Acts 2:38-39; 16:30-31).
3. I should remember that all the Bible stories and all its history of individuals and nations have been written for MY warning, MY encouragement, or MY learning, and I should not stop reading till I get the lesson for my own heart (1 Cor. 10:5-13).
4. I should meditate or think about what I have read in the Bible and talk about it to others (Josh. 1:8; Ps. 1:2).

5. When I read the Bible, I should get a dictionary and find the meaning of every word or seek someone to explain what I do not understand. I should get a reference Bible and a concordance, learn how to use them, and USE THEM in the study of the Bible (Acts 8:30-31).

6. God talks to me when I read the Bible. I talk to God when I pray. I should let God do most of the talking.

7. When I read the Bible, I must expect that the Holy Spirit will be my Teacher. The Holy Spirit wrote the Bible (John 14:26; 2 Pet. 1:21).

THE BIBLE AND THE MISSIONARY CAUSE

The Bible is a foreign mission book, and Christianity is a foreign missionary religion. To be anti-missionary in spirit is to be anti-Christian in spirit. Dr. William Adams Brown enumerated 14 points in which the Bible supports foreign missions. What a wonderful book the Bible is! We have never scaled its heights nor sounded its depths. New light is constantly flashing from it. The Christian world is indebted to Dr. Brown for these 14 points which he dug out of the Bible.

1. Every book in the New Testament was written by a foreign missionary.

2. Every epistle in the New Testament that was written to a church was written to a foreign missionary church.

3. Every letter in the New Testament that was written to an individual was written to the convert of a foreign missionary.

4. Every book in the New Testament that was written to a community of believers was written to a group of foreign missionary churches.

5. The one book of prophecy in the New Testament was written to the seven foreign missionary churches in Asia.

6. The only authoritative history of the early Christian church is a foreign missionary journal.

7. The disciples were called Christians first in a foreign missionary community.

8. The language of the books of the New Testament is the missionary's language.

9. The map of the early Christians world traces the missionary journeys of the apostles.

10. The problems which arose in the early Church were largely questions of missionary procedure.

11. Of the Twelve Apostles chosen by Jesus, every Apostle except one became a missionary.

12. The only man among the Twelve Apostles who did not become a missionary became a traitor.

13. Only a foreign missionary could write an everlasting Gospel.

14. According to the Apostles, the missionary is the highest expression of the Christian life.

YOUR OWN BIBLE

1. Get one with plain print, as you should with any other book.
2. Get it for use, not show.
3. Use it daily.
4. Commit it to memory, one verse every day.
5. Read it through, a book at a time.
6. Think about it as you are engaged in your work.
7. Talk about it with your friends.
8. Practice its precepts in your everyday life.
9. Pray for strength to follow its commands.
10. Help others to find in it the same joy that you have.

HOW BEST TO ACQUIRE KNOWLEDGE OF THE BIBLE

1. Have a good, plain type Bible, a concordance, Bible textbook, and, if possible, one good commentary and a book about biblical history. An understandable version of the Bible should also be at hand.

2. Read the Bible consistently, extensively, and regularly, seeking to become thoroughly familiar with the book as a whole.

3. Mark the passages that impress you, and, in a notebook, jot down matters for special study and also such thoughts as may be valuable.

4. Become thoroughly familiar with the historic and geographic setting of the biblical narrative.

5. Make a special study of separate books, noting particularly the occasion, purpose, characteristics, and doctrines of the books.

6. Study topics, comparing scripture with scripture. Read also what the best writers have to say about these subjects.

7. Commit to memory a great deal of God's Word. No other habit will more thoroughly enrich your mind.

8. Seek the truth in order to use it. Make it the rule and support of your own life and the means of leading others to the blessings of salvation.

9. Beware of irreverence in the treatment of God's Word. Scripture should not be the object or vehicle of jest nor treated with a familiarity which breeds contempt.

HOW TO STUDY THE BIBLE
By: Dwight L. Moody

I never saw a useful Christian who was not a student of the Bible. If a man neglects his Bible, he may pray and ask God to use him, but there is not much for the Holy Spirit to work with. We must have the Word itself, which is sharper than any two-edged sword.

The sermon spoken by Moses before he left the children of Israel was just a rehearsal of what God had done for them, and when Peter stood up on the Day of Pentecost, the Scripture he quoted to the people was the arrow that went down into their hearts and explained the Scripture from the time of Abraham downward.

People are constantly saying, "We want something new—some new doctrine, some new idea." Depend upon it, if you get tired of the Word of God and it becomes worrisome to you, you are out of communion with Him. What you need is someone who will unfold and expound the Scriptures to you.

There is no situation in life for which you cannot find some word of consolation in Scripture. If you are in affliction or in adversity, if you are in joy or sorrow, in health or in sickness, in riches or in poverty, in any condition of life—God has a promise stored up in His Word for you.

Perhaps, you ask, "How can I fall in love with the Bible?" Well, if you will only rouse yourself to the study of it and ask God's assistance, He will assuredly help you. There are three books which I think every Christian ought to possess. The first, of course, is the Bible. I believe in getting a good Bible, with clear print. Perhaps you say that you cannot carry a big Bible in your pocket. Well, carry it under your arm—and if you walk five miles, you will be preaching a sermon five miles long. I know a man who was converted by seeing someone carrying his Bible under his arm.

If you get a good Bible, you are likely to take better care of it. The older you grow, the more precious it will become to you. But be sure you do not get one so good that you will be afraid to mark. Then, get a concordance and a Bible textbook. These books will help you study the Word of God with profit. If you do not have them, get them tomorrow, for every Christian should own them.

Topical Study

One of the best ways to study the Scriptures is to study them topically. At one time, I would read a certain number of chapters a day. If I did not, I thought I was getting cold and backsliding. But if a man had asked me two hours afterwards what I had read, I could not have told him. Merely reading the Bible is no use at all unless we study it thoroughly. Read as if you were seeking for something of value. It is a good deal better to take a single chapter and spend a month on it than to read the Bible at random for a month.

I looked up the word *love*, and I do not know how many weeks I spent in studying the messages in which it occurs. At last I could not help loving people. I had been feeding so long on love that I was anxious to do good to everybody I came in contact with. Study "Grace," study "Faith," and study "Assurance." Some people do not believe in assurance. Paul said: "I know that my Redeemer lives." It is not "I hope," or "I think."

The best book on assurance is John's first epistle. Sometimes, a book of the Bible will contain a verse which is a sort of key to the book, and which unfolds it. In John 20:31, we read, "These are written, that ye might believe that Jesus is the Christ, the Son of God; and that believing ye might have life through his name" (KJV). But in 1 John 5:13, we read, "These things have I written unto you that believe on the name of the Son of God; that ye may know that ye have eternal life, and that ye may believe on the name of the Son of God" (KJV). That whole epistle is written on assurance.

I have heard some people say it was not their privilege to know that they were saved. They had heard a minister say that no one can know whether he is saved or not, and they took what the minister said instead of what the Word of God says. If you will just take up your Bible and study assurance for a week, you will find it is your privilege to know that you are a child of God.

The Promise

Take the promise of God. Let a man feed for a month on the promises of God, and he will not talk about how poor he is. You hear people say, "Oh, my leanness! How lean I am!" It is not their leanness; it is their laziness. If you would only read from Genesis to Revelation and see all the promises made by God to Abraham, to Isaac, to Jacob, to the Jews, and to the Gentiles, and to all His people—if you would spend a month feeding on the previous promises of God—you would not be going about complaining how poor you are. You would lift up your head and proclaim the riches of His grace, because you could not help doing it.

Spend a month at Prayer. Then take up Hope, Faith, and Grace, and feed on them. The Bible will become a new book to you.

Another way is to study one book at a time. For instance, Genesis is the seed-pot of the whole Bible. It tells us of life, death, and resurrection; it involves all the rest of the Bible.

Or study a single word that runs through a book. I was wonderfully blessed by studying the seven "blessings" of Revelation. If you take up the eight "overcomes" of Revelation, you will find them a fruitful subject. They take you right up to heaven; you climb by them right up to the throne of God.

Then, there is the word "know," for example. It occurs six times in 1 John 3. Some people tell us that what we believe does not make any difference and that a lie is as good as the truth if only we are sincere. No doubt the false prophets on Mount Carmel were sincere, but John says, "Hereby we know that we are of the truth." Then, "We know that we have passed from death unto life, because we love the brethren." There is assurance for you!

The Christian is not full of jealousy, envy, hatred, and malice. He is full of "love, joy, peace, long-suffering, gentleness, goodness, faith, meekness, temperance." These are the fruits I shall bear if I have Christ in me. That fifth chapter of Galatians will soon tell us if we have that right kind of fruit. Make the tree right, and you will soon have the right fruit.

I have also been greatly blessed by studying the "believers" in John. He wrote his gospel that we might believe. All through it is "believe, believe, believe." If you want to persuade a man that Christ is the Son of God, John is the Gospel for him. Matthew was a Jew, and he writes of Christ as a Jew—as the Son of David coming to take His throne. He commences with Abraham, and speaks of the kingdom all the way down to Christ. Mark begins with Malachi. He takes up where the Old Testament left off and speaks of Christ as a servant coming to do the will of God. Luke takes up the human side and speaks of Christ as a physician, healing the sick. But John brings Christ out of the bosom of the Father. He goes beyond Malachi, beyond Abraham, beyond Adam, beyond the morning stars, and brings Christ out of the Father's bosom, and with one stroke of the pen, settles the question of Unitarianism forever. John says the Son of God was manifest in the flesh.

Notes

Notes

Notes

Notes